International Wealth Success was founded by Tyler G. Hicks in 1966 to empower and educate people everywhere on successful wealth building. Every book, kit, guide, and directory is guaranteed to offer proven strategies and actionable insights to help you achieve your financial, business, and personal goals. Turn the page and start right here, right now...

The road to financial freedom begins with education and the courage to take action.

~ Tyler G. Hicks

PRAISE FOR TYLER G. HICKS AND IW$

ATTAINING A GOAL

*"**Using info from your publications** I recently obtained a loan to start a toy distributor business with little difficulty. I am achieving a goal."*

HIS FIRST $1,000,000

*"**Using your ideas and methods**, and especially your down-to-earth advice and guidance on real estate negotiations, I have been able to acquire 2 properties and I am well on my way to my first $1-million through two sources—real estate and an Internet advertising company."*

MAKING GOOD MONEY IN PART TIME

*"As of today, I am pulling a minimum of $19,000 per month in fees, and **increasing my earnings every month**. I expect to go full-time in this business next month as a Professional Financial Broker."*

VALUABLE CONTACTS

*"Through the **IWS Newsletter ATTAIN** I formed my own corporation and made a number of valuable international contacts that have been most profitable. **I quit my job to devote full time to my business ventures.**"*

BIG DEAL FOR A CLIENT

*"By the way, **using your techniques**, we did assist our client in overcoming the largest hurdle for his deal—the $10-million firm commitment from the lender in the first position mortgage."*

A NEW CAREER

*"I retired from the NFL nine years ago and **your book on real estate has kept the big money coming in!**"*

VENTURE CAPITAL SUCCESS

*"I negotiated a $100,000 venture capital loan through the ad I ran in **the IWS Newsletter ATTAIN**. Thank you!"*

Other books in the IW$ Guide Series

The IW$ Guide to Product Licensing Success
The IW$ Guide to Affiliate Marketing
The IW$ Guide to Franchise Success
The IW$ Guide to How to Buy a Business with No Money Down

The IW$ Directory Series

The IW$ Directory of Business Capital Sources
The IW$ Directory of Startup, Seed, and Equity Capital Sources

More books by Tyler G. Hicks

Tyler G. Hicks Wealth Creation Vault
The Leverage Code

More books, complete kits, and entrepreneurial advisory at *iWealthSuccess.com.*

Move forward boldly!

The IW$ Guide to

Rural Real Estate

SUCCEED AND PROSPER BUYING AND SELLING COUNTRY LAND

Frank E. Moss, Ph.D.

Tyler G. Hicks

International Wealth Success (IW$)

IW$ PRESS

Wilkes-Barre, PA

IW$
PRESS

ISBN-13 978-1-964205-20-5

10 9 8 7 6 5 4 3 2 1

IW$ Press is an imprint of Kallisti Publishing Inc., whose titles may be bulk purchased for business or promotional use or for special sales. Please see *https://www.IWSPress.com* for more information.

For any lexicographers or philologists into whose hands this book may fall, the publisher may or may not have incorporated into the text, as a stimulus and a challenge to your perspicacity, one or more deliberate errors. If you'd like to alert us to your discovery, please visit https://*readKP.com/typo*.

DESIGNED IN THE UNITED STATES

CONTENTS

Want to be flooded with really big money, millions and up? Then come with me while I show you how to latch onto the megabucks! Many of my readers have done just that, today. And they winter in the Virgin Islands, swimming off their palatial yachts when they feel like it. You, I'm convinced, can do the same.

~ Tyler G. Hicks

INTRODUCTION

Your Road to Rural Real Estate Success

There are moments in history when the right course becomes quietly obvious to those who take the time to look. Not obvious in the sense of headlines or popular enthusiasm, but obvious in the deeper sense—when long-standing forces align, when patterns repeat, and when opportunity presents itself in a form that rewards patience, intelligence, and independence.

Country land investing exists squarely in that category.

This book is written for people who value clarity over noise, substance over fashion, and results over theory. It is written for those who understand that wealth built carefully tends to endure, and that independence gained deliberately tends to compound. It is written for people who wish to step outside crowded paths and operate where competition is thinner, terms are friendlier, and time itself becomes an ally.

Land has occupied a central place in the accumulation of wealth for as long as ownership has existed. Empires rose on it. Families secured their futures through it. Entire civilizations measured prosperity by control of it. Across centuries and continents, land has remained the one asset whose importance never faded, even as currencies, technologies, and institutions changed around it.

That permanence matters.

Unlike manufactured goods, land does not wear out. Unlike businesses, it does not require daily management. Unlike paper assets, it does not depend on confidence alone. Land exists. It endures. It holds value across generations because it satisfies enduring human needs: space, shelter, resources, and freedom of use.

Yet within the broad category of land ownership, country land occupies a special position—one that is consistently underestimated.

Country land is often overlooked because it appears quiet. It lacks the drama of urban development and the apparent sophistication of commercial projects. It does not generate monthly rent checks or glossy brochures. Its virtues unfold slowly, steadily, and with remarkable reliability. That very quality has kept it accessible long after other forms of real estate became crowded, expensive, and institutionally dominated.

This book concerns itself with that overlooked advantage.

It explains why country land has produced exceptional results for ordinary individuals working part time. It shows how appreciation occurs, how leverage multiplies outcomes, and how timing and distance shape value in ways that can be measured and used. It demonstrates how ownership can be achieved with modest capital—and in certain circumstances, with almost none at all.

The methods described here do not rely on speculation. They do not depend on perfect foresight or rare genius. They rely on observation, structure, and discipline. They reward those who understand that wealth accumulation resembles farming more than gambling: prepare the ground, plant carefully, allow time to work, and harvest deliberately.

Country land rewards that approach better than almost any other investment category available today.

One reason lies in its financing.

Owner financing remains common in country land transactions. Sellers often prefer steady income over a lump sum. They value simplicity over institutional complexity. This creates opportunities for buyers to secure long terms, reasonable interest rates, and modest down payments—conditions that amplify leverage and accelerate equity growth. In contrast, many other investment arenas impose rigid terms, institutional oversight, and frequent renegotiation.

Another reason lies in demand patterns.

People move first. Prices follow. Country land sits at the frontier of that movement. As cities expand and populations seek space, privacy, and autonomy, the pressure moves outward. What was once considered remote becomes desirable. What was once idle becomes valuable. These shifts follow patterns that can be studied, measured, and anticipated.

Time and distance analysis—the subject of several chapters in this book—transforms those patterns into practical tools. By examining how prices behave relative to urban centers and over time, investors gain insight unavailable to casual observers. This insight allows purchases to occur before demand becomes obvious and sales to occur after value has matured.

That difference in timing accounts for much of the profit potential discussed in these pages.

Country land also offers something that many other investments cannot: usability.

Owners enjoy their land while they hold it. Hunting, fishing, hiking, timber management, firewood production, small-scale agriculture, and simple retreat all become part of ownership. This use adds personal value and often increases market appeal. In contrast, many financial assets offer no such return during the holding period.

There is also a psychological advantage.

Country land ownership fosters a sense of control and independence that extends beyond financial statements. It represents autonomy in a literal sense—control over space, resources, and decisions. For many people, this sense of control carries weight equal to monetary gain. It aligns investment with lifestyle rather than separating the two.

This book does not promise instant results.

What it offers instead is something far more valuable: a coherent system. A system that explains how value forms, how leverage functions, how risk is managed, and how capital can be recycled repeatedly through intelligent buying and selling. It provides tools rather than tricks, principles rather than formulas.

You will learn how to recognize bargains, how to negotiate terms, how to structure financing, and how to understand contracts without intimidation. You will see how profits compound through pyramiding, how zero-cash deals arise, and how options and timing can produce extraordinary percentage returns under the right conditions.

You will also learn restraint.

Country land investing rewards those who wait for the right moment. Buying too early ties up capital. Buying too late compresses returns. Selling at the right time converts paper gains into usable capital. The discipline to act selectively and decisively distinguishes success from frustration.

Throughout this book, real examples anchor the discussion. These are not hypothetical illustrations designed to impress. They are ordinary transactions executed by ordinary people who followed sound procedures. Their power lies in their repeatability.

One theme appears again and again: homework.

The most profitable opportunities arise where information is unevenly distributed. The investor who studies zoning, infrastructure plans, population movement, and comparable sales sees possibilities invisible to others. That informational advantage transforms uncertainty into opportunity.

Another theme is leverage.

Leverage magnifies outcomes when used thoughtfully. It allows control of valuable property with limited capital. It accelerates equity growth when appreciation occurs. It rewards patience and penalizes haste. Used correctly, it becomes a multiplier rather than a risk.

Country land provides an ideal environment for leverage because financing terms often remain fixed while values rise. This creates a widening gap between obligation and worth—a gap that translates into wealth.

This book also emphasizes simplicity.

Complexity often masquerades as sophistication. In practice, it frequently obscures risk. Country land transactions tend to involve fewer parties, fewer variables, and fewer surprises. Clear contracts, fixed terms, and tangible assets replace layers of abstraction.

That simplicity favors individuals.

Large institutions thrive in environments that require scale, bureaucracy, and constant management. Country land favors those willing to observe carefully, negotiate directly, and act independently. It remains one of the few arenas where part-time effort can still produce outsized results.

The chapters that follow build logically.

You will begin with fundamental concepts: value, demand, supply, timing, and distance. You will move through bargaining, financing, and strategy. You will examine documents, contracts, and structures. You will explore zero-cash opportunities and options. Finally, you will see how these elements combine into a coherent philosophy of wealth, security, and independence.

Each chapter stands on its own, yet each supports the whole.

The goal is not merely to inform, but to equip.

When you finish this book, you will see land differently. You will understand why certain parcels attract demand while others languish. You will recognize opportunities earlier. You will negotiate with greater confidence. You will evaluate deals with clarity rather than hope.

Most importantly, you will possess a framework that remains useful across changing economic conditions.

Inflation rises and falls. Interest rates fluctuate. Policies shift. Yet land endures. Its supply remains limited. Its demand renews itself. Those who understand this—and act accordingly—place themselves in a position of long-term advantage.

Country land investing is not a shortcut.

It is a path.

A path that rewards thoughtfulness, discipline, and independence. A path that allows progress without haste and wealth without fragility. A path open to those willing to study, to act, and to allow time to do its work.

If that appeals to you, then you are holding the right book.

The chapters ahead will show you how.

THE
IW$ GUIDE
TO
RURAL
REAL
ESTATE

All you need is one salable activity to pursue in your spare time and you can become comfortably rich.

~ Tyler G. Hicks

CHAPTER 1

IMPROVING YOUR LIFESTYLE

New Dimensions for Wealthier, Healthier, and Safer Living

What do you want out of life?

- More wealth?
- Greater admiration and respect from family, friends, and neighbors?
- Better health, including purer, healthier foods to eat and air to breathe?
- More safety, not only physical safety, but better protection for your newly acquired wealth, and a more secure future for your children?
- More fun?
- Freedom?

These are the things that most people want and work hard for all their lives. But only a few people actually achieve them. I would like to show you here that it is easier than you think to become one of these few survivors.

My wife and I began a modest investment program several years ago, designed to acquire country land. Our program has provided us with many of the items listed above. As a result of our experiences, we are convinced that country land is one of the easiest, safest, and most successful investments that ordinary people can make in order to gain more wealth and better security—especially in years of economic danger and uncertainty.

We want to share our experiences with you in this book. Please read it carefully. We know that if you adopt even a few of the many suggestions given here, your lifestyle will be improved.

FIRST, A FEW QUESTIONS FOR YOU

Before we get into it, let me ask you:

1. Are you a survivalist?
2. Can you set a goal for yourself and work steadily toward it?
3. One who can determine your own lifestyle, without having to follow the lead of your neighbors?
4. Do you sincerely want to improve the quality of your life and increase your standard of living?

Please look at this next question carefully. It's an important one.

5. Can you do without a new car for the next few years?

If your answer to these questions is "yes," then you are what I might call a survivalist—most especially the last one—because I will show you how you can acquire at least 10 acres of country land—and possibly as much as 40—for about what it would cost you to buy a new, mid-priced car. It is even possible, under the proper circumstances, to gain control of country property with no down payment at all—and even to sell it for a profit a short time later.

I have done this, and I will show you how. And you will discover many other things as well . . .

WHAT YOU NEED TO KNOW IN ORDER TO SURVIVE . . .

. . . and even thrive:

- How to make your pleasures profitable to you.
- How we did it, and how you can too.
- Why country land investments are safer.
- What is inflation—and how it can destroy your standard of living.

- What causes inflation—and why it is certain to return.
- How deficits in the Federal Budget can savage you—and what to do about it.
- How the uncontrollable, double-digit inflation in natural gas prices can work to your advantage—if you own some woodland.
- How to make your land "income-producing"—and the very positive effect of that on its worth.
- How to estimate the value of a piece of land—and what you can do to increase it.
- The all-important role of location—and how to avoid a common trap: buying in the wrong place.
- How living and working in a large city can act in your favor once you've learned to find the "preferred directions of growth."
- How to search for and find a bargain.
- Successful negotiating techniques—these are most important.
- Inside knowledge—and how to obtain it.
- Time/Distance analysis: how to use it to your great advantage.
- What about vacation land? Some of the best profits are here and you can really enjoy it while constantly adding to your net worth.
- How to finance land purchases. The critical importance of leverage—and how to use it effectively.
- Why you should not pay cash—even if you can.
- How to use buying and selling strategies effectively.
- How "pyramiding" can work to potentially speed up your accumulation of wealth.
- All about writing contracts.
- All about deeds, notes, closing statements, and other instruments.

- How deals are made with zero cash. So important, that one whole chapter of this book is devoted to this topic alone.
- Why country land is your best bet for increasing your net worth.

. . . and a final word . . .

- How your library can help: what are the best books on country land.

You will learn all of this, and much, much more in the following chapters of this book.

CHAPTER 2

ACQUIRE WEALTH AND HAVE FUN DOING IT

Do You Enjoy Being Outdoors? Then This Is For You

Most people assume that they should pay for having fun. Vacations and weekends cost money.

But a few smart people—usually wealthy people—seem to have found ways to make money even from their vacations or hobbies. There is a well-known coffee magnate who likes to go on African safaris. He produces promotional material for his company while in Africa. That, of course, makes his trip a business expense, rather than a luxury vacation.

There is absolutely nothing wrong with this. The creation of promotional material is a very real and necessary business expense.

The question is: *how to apply this same idea to your particular lifestyle.* If you enjoy the outdoors—camping, hiking, fishing, hunting, and similar pleasures—then you can quite easily make these pastimes pay for themselves. For the same price that you might pay for a couple of vacations, you can actually acquire a country property on which you can do many of these same things. After a few years, you may sell your land for a nice profit: your vacations were "free!"

MAKING PLEASURE PAY

There are two distinct ways to approach the question of making your land pay some or all of your expenses. They depend on whether you regard your land as an investment or as a business.

As an **investment**, you simply are regarding your land in the same manner as some stocks or bonds you might own.

You hope to sell them later at a profit. However, the cost of any improvements which you make on the land will be deductible from your profits when you sell.

Are you cutting wood to burn in your fireplace or wood stove? No, you are thinning the forest, and thereby improving your land. Your expenses are a legitimate cost associated with your investment. Here are a few other possibilities for land improvements:

1. **Plant trees.** You can frequently obtain the seedlings free from the U.S. Department of Agriculture or from your state conservation department. Consult your local USDA office for details.
2. **Put in a lake.** Again, local USDA or state conservation offices can help. They can often assist with planning and fish stocking.
3. **Improve pastures, cut brush, improve or install fencing.**
4. **Add or improve roads.**

Other suggestions for improvements will be found in Chapter 8.

MAKE IT A BUSINESS

If you can make some income—even a small income—from your property, all your expenses incurred in producing that income become business expenses, and are deductible from profits. In Chapter 7, there is a detailed plan for operating two businesses—woodheat and wildflower businesses—from your land. The possibilities for making a small income are almost endless.

Best of all, many of these activities can actually improve the quality of your own life as well. Here are some possibilities with comments where appropriate:

1. **Beekeeping.** Do you like honey? Many people think it's better for you than sugar. Sell the excess to a

health food store. Beekeeping, once established, does not require a lot of time, and it's supposed to be fun.

2. **Check your fences, and talk a neighbor into co-operative cattle raising.** You will have much better quality beef for your own table, and you can profit from the rest. *Caution:* daily attention is required. Either you or the neighbor should live next to the land.
3. **Rent the pasture, the crop land, or the hunting rights.** These are the easiest of all, and require practically no time or attention.
4. **Grow ginseng.** This is one of the most interesting and profitable crops right now. Would you believe that the largest market for this natural food and remedy is in Asia, but the world's largest supplier is North America? There is a very large demand for this unusual root and currently there is a short supply. See Chapter 5 for a discussion of what this does to prices, then check those prices at your neighborhood health food store. It even grows wild over some parts of America, so keep an eye out for it when inspecting property to buy.
5. **Plant a "Christmas tree" farm.** This business is becoming extremely profitable. Surprise! You can get the seedlings for almost nothing from many state conservation services.

The variety of this short list will give you some idea of the possibilities. Your own imagination can supply many more.

Be sure to check frequently with your local USDA or state conservation office. If your "farm" is "income-producing," as opposed to simply idle land, it may qualify for a number of Department of Agriculture grants and subsidies.

And also, always remember one thing: any improvements or additions which produce income (even small income) make your property instantly much more valuable and attractive to prospective buyers.

CHAPTER 3

WE DID IT!

And You Can Too!

Elaine (my wife) and I—we did it. As you read on, we'll show you how. I am a college science professor, and Elaine teaches in a daycare center. We had modest incomes and no particular expertise in the realm of real estate investments.

With a lot of scrimping early on, we had managed to acquire a second house, which we rented. Investing in rental property is a headache—there's always something to be fixed, like the furnace on the coldest day of winter, or a leaky roof during a summer deluge, and there are renters who don't pay, vacate early without telling you, wreck the place during boisterous parties, etc.

Several years earlier, we had had enough of that, and so decided to sell the house. We had an offer which gave us a very comfortable profit, so we accepted it, and for a time we were flush with cash. At the same time, we were planning a study leave in Europe which would last a year and a half.

We wondered what to do with our money to protect its buying power while we were away. Some of our friends advised buying a small apartment building, but we already knew too much about the rental business. Besides, imagine arranging to have the furnace fixed (instantly, if not sooner!) in the dead of winter from 6,000 miles away!

We even thought about buying gold. At the time, it would have been a disaster! It was selling in the range of $650 per ounce when we left for Europe, and even though it did rise dramatically to near $850 per ounce while we were there, it had plunged (not so dramatically) to a low of around $375 within six months after we had returned. A similar performance would have been true of most other investments as well.

Certainly these were not for ordinary people like us. Even today, we can't remember which one of us had the bright idea to buy some country land.

SHOULD WE BUY A SMALL FARM OR SOME WOODLAND?

After all, its value would keep up with the inflation rate, and if we were lucky, maybe even beat it. Certainly nothing could happen to it while we were gone. And best of all—no renters to worry about, no insurance to buy, and no expensive real estate taxes to pay.

The wildlife would enjoy it while we were gone, and it would all be there waiting for us when we returned—just as we left it, except that the trees and bushes would have grown some. And then, maybe we could enjoy it some too. We had always enjoyed camping and hiking. Later, we discovered many ways in which owning a piece of country land can improve the quality of your life and enhance your lifestyle—ways that we want to share with you as you read through this book. But meanwhile, let's return to our first deal.

We were right in our reasoning about the safety and convenience of a land investment, but that didn't become obvious until much later. And we were incredibly lucky with our first deal. We found a very pretty 65-acre parcel near a small country town. The asking price was $750 per acre. We offered $700 (we knew nothing about land values at that point) and the seller finally compromised at $727.

In addition, the seller agreed to accept only 25% down, and to finance the remainder for 10 years at 9% interest. It seemed quite a good deal to us—and it was! Because, within two weeks, we were approached by a real estate agent who informed us that he had a buyer for our land. The prospective buyer was a builder who thought our property was ideal for development.

$4,000 PROFIT IN TWO MONTHS WITH NO MONEY INVESTED!

Too good to be true? Well it happened to us this way.

The buyer offered $850 per acre—and we accepted. We had not even closed on the purchase yet. The only thing we had done was to sign a contract with our seller and attach to it an "earnest money" check for $500, which he could not cash until after closing.

On a certain day we had two closings:

- with our seller (when we bought the land for $727) in the morning, and
- with our buyer (when we sold it for $850) that same afternoon.

After paying the agent's fee, we had made a clear profit of very nearly $4,000—without having invested a penny! (Agent's fees are normally 10% of the sale price, and the seller pays. In this case, however, the agent was so anxious to put the deal through, that he agreed to a 50/50 split of the profit.)

Well! That doesn't happen every day, but the possibility of finding a similar "gold mine" every now and then is enough to make investing in country land the most exciting and interesting part-time occupation (honestly, it's more like a hobby) we could think of.

SOLD ON COUNTRY LAND

After that, we were "sold" on investing in country land, as you can well imagine. Early on, however, we were rank amateurs. And we were suffering from a severe case of overenthusiasm—usually the right ingredients for a disaster, had we been investing in anything else.

We did make some mistakes afterwards, fortunately none very costly. And that's one of the best things about country land: *it's forgiving.*

It's nearly impossible for a person of reasonable common sense and caution to actually lose money, although a poor initial choice of property or the payment of too high a price may cause you to have to wait several years for a reasonable profit—assuming that profit is your motive.

In spite of our mistakes, we have accumulated holdings conservatively valued at more than $120,000 today—and that does not include our house or a substantial cash reserve. Not bad, considering that we started only a few years ago with about $12,000 cash from the sale of our rental house.

Back then, we were "wage slaves." Today, we have substantial net worth. We still continue to teach, because we enjoy it; and we can do so, because our land transactions do not require much time or effort. In fact, our "land business" is more like a hobby. Nearly every required activity is enjoyable and, in addition, we use our land very frequently for recreational pleasures—that's the big dividend.

Remember that we are just ordinary people, so you can do this, too! And you don't need a huge pile of money to get started. Fortunately, country land comes in all sizes, shapes, and price ranges. You can start for as little as a new car would cost, or even with no money at all, as with our first deal.

Regardless of whether you wish to profit from a multitude of transactions, or simply to acquire a country place of your own to enjoy over the years, we are convinced that YOU CAN DO IT TOO.

CHAPTER 4

SAFER THAN YOUR OWN HOME

History Shows That Country Land Is Unsurpassed as a Safe Store of Value

The best and safest investment for the average American over the past three decades has been his home! Right?

Absolutely correct. The average American homeowner gained substantial capital worth from his home. He could have made no other investment during that decade which would have provided the same or better protection, safety, and appreciation of value.

Wrong! Country land, even a modestly priced, carefully chosen, smaller parcel, would have outperformed the average house, both for safety and for capital appreciation.

WHAT THE RECORD SAYS ABOUT CAPITAL APPRECIATION

As the chart below shows, the average existing house gained an average of 17% per year over a seven-year period. Not bad at all compared to almost any other investment that an ordinary person could have made. This chart reflects a specific historical period and is shown to illustrate long-term trends in relative performance—not to suggest identical results in every future cycle.

In fact, that average 17% appreciation in home values has made the generation of Americans who bought well-located, quality housing, in say 1968 or 1970, quite wealthy today, at least on paper, and insofar as their home is concerned.

The price of farmland (in dollars per acre) compared to the price of an existing family house (in dollars), and the average annual gain (percent per year).[1]

Year	Farmland	House
1973	246	32,900
1975	339	39,900
1977	448	47,900
1979	559	63,700
1980	677	72,000
Gain	25%/yr.	17%/yr.

But that 17% appreciation in average, existing housing seems pretty miserly compared to the whopping 25% per year ticked up by the average acre of U. S. farmland. And you must remember, that's only the average performance. With a little effort and some time spent in studying the market, you should be able to beat the average performance by a good margin. Even where you live can make a great deal of difference.

Please note that while the figures shown here come from the 1970s, more recent decades have continued to show strong long-term appreciation in well-located farmland and rural land, particularly during periods of inflation and monetary expansion. The principle remains the same: land's limited supply and essential utility support its value over time.

In certain states, Illinois and Iowa for example, the average annual gain for the same period of time approached 36%, and near some large metropolitan areas, even more. So if you are located in a large city, the odds are that you can do better than the average performance, simply because of your location alone. So supposing that future economic conditions resemble those shown in the preceding chart, you can easily

1 The prices are averages for the entire U.S. Farmland prices are from the U.S. Department of Agriculture, Research Bureau, and the house prices are from the National Association of Realtors.

profit and protect the value of your money by owning some country land.

AND A WORD ABOUT SAFETY

Very little, excepting floods and forest fires, can happen to country land. And if your land is at all well chosen, you don't need to worry about floods. By contrast, if you owned an apartment building, you would have to worry about, and in most cases insure yourself against a whole host of possible catastrophes: fire, vandalism, irresponsible and destructive tenants, roof and plumbing leaks, owner's liabilities, and many others. In addition to this, you might have to bear frequent and unexpected increases in (already large!) property taxes, whereas the country land owner would probably see only modest increases in (very low) taxes.

AND PRICE STABILITY

One of the great advantages of a country land investment, as compared to other investments, is price stability. That is: the tendency of land prices to avoid wild swings, often under the influence of unanticipated and uncontrollable events. All consumable commodities, like potatoes, wheat, and soybeans, are subject to many market forces which greatly affect the price. Probably the strongest and most unpredictable of these is the weather. Even stocks, and to a lesser extent bonds, show rapid and sometimes severe price reactions to specific and often uncontrolled economic and business factors.

It's better to leave these investments to the professionals. But as the chart shows, the very healthy price rises in country land have been slow and steady. In addition, there is another very safe characteristic: even in a poor market, the price tends to avoid large decreases.

Instead, it seems to "stick" at or near the last level where land was traded. This feature is mentioned again in more detail in the next chapter. Of course there are exceptions to this general behavior, but they have been few and far between, and largely confined to special locations. "Booms" followed by "busts" in land prices have occasionally occurred: most notably in Florida in the 1920's and a century earlier in Chicago. These strange "happenings" were fed by unscrupulous land speculators selling their holdings to large numbers of naive and unknowledgeable people. By carefully following this guide, especially Chapters 8–11, you should be able to easily avoid any such trap.

CHAPTER 5

SUPPLY AND DEMAND

"They Don't Make It Anymore!"

The law of supply and demand is perhaps the oldest law of the marketplace. It simply states that if a certain commodity or manufactured item or service is in short supply at the same time that there is a great and increasing demand, then the price for that commodity, item, or service must increase.

Happy is the person who owns a large quantity of anything which comes into great demand. Sometimes, if the demand is great enough and the supply short enough, he can name his own price. On the other hand, a wise investor must avoid getting caught with an oversupply of anything as the demand is drying up. The price then will surely go down—and buyers will be hard to find.

The behavior of the precious metals—gold and silver—is a good example. During a period of steadily growing inflation commencing in 1972 and ending with the raging 17% rates which occurred in 1980, gold and silver were in constantly increasing demand and ever-tightening supply. This drove the price of gold to an all-time high of around $860 per ounce, and silver to nearly $55 per ounce.

However, in 1981 and 1982, as many investors who had been holding large quantities released these for sale, and as South Africa and the Soviet Union flooded the market with large quantities, the price dramatically dropped to lows of around $345 and $5.80 in early 1982.

My purpose here is simply to illustrate the action of supply and demand on the price of gold and silver. In the next chapter, I will discuss the action of inflation more completely, and show you why country land is an excellent investment in inflationary times.

THE SUPPLY OF AND DEMAND FOR LAND

The law of supply and demand works equally well in establishing the price of land, with one important modification. As the caption above indicates, the supply of land overall cannot be increased. It cannot be manufactured or mined or otherwise "made." People want—or demand—land. They want it for many purposes: to build houses on, to grow food on, to hunt, hike or vacation on—and also simply to invest in—often holding on to it indefinitely after acquisition—and by doing so, further reducing the supply. And the number of people in the world, and in every country, is ever increasing.

In the long run, the demand for land is always increasing over the supply. The price is, therefore, bound to go up, even without the assistance of inflation. In places where the population density, the number of people living per square mile, is very high, then the demand, and hence the price of land, is also very high.

Europe and England are examples where the population density is nearly twice as large as the United States. Land there is so tightly held, and in such demand, that in acre quantities only the wealthy class can afford to own it.

Indeed, we in the United States are lucky. As I shall show you in this book, anyone can acquire and own land—often more easily than you can buy a car.

Of course, there are local variations in the strength of demand and the adequacy of supply, as shown by the number of land owners willing to sell their land. Demand is greatest and prices increase most sharply in those areas where the local population density is increasing most rapidly—popular places to live, work, or vacation as well as places where people are moving in. According to the 1980 census, one of the most rapidly growing regions in the country was the Olympic Peninsula in Washington State—average land prices there have approximately quadrupled in only the last six years.

There are, of course, counterexamples: places where the population density is not increasing or may actually be decreasing. In such places, demand for land may have dried up, while at the same time there are many would-be sellers.

Unlike commodities (gold or potatoes, for example) the price of land in abundant supply does not often "collapse." Instead, the market simply remains idle for a time, and prices have a tendency to "stick" near their last levels. This situation will remain until demand catches up with supply.

As I shall show in later chapters, this will often happen due to factors other than population increases. Prices most often become "unstuck" and begin to rise sharply in response to increasing inflation rates. It is this "stickiness," or the tendency of prices to resist downward pressure in times of oversupply, that makes country land an extremely safe investment for the average person.

DEMAND NEAR A METRO AREA—ALWAYS INCREASING

People who live and work in metropolitan areas have a tendency to always push toward the suburbs. They want a better house, farther away from the problems of the cities, and more land around it. It seems to always be true that "farther out and larger" is always "better." Even the high prices for automobiles and fuel, which have occurred largely since 1978, have not seemed to dampen this demand.

This, coupled with the fact that the population of nearly all metropolitan areas is continuing to increase, has created an unparalleled demand for country land within commuting distance of large cities. And this growing demand shows no signs of slowing up in the future. There are many reasons which account for increasing demand, which I shall discuss in detail in Chapters 8, 9, and 11.

ENERGY PRICES CREATE WOODLAND DEMAND

In Chapter 7, I will show you how to operate a wood heat business from as little as 10 acres of woodland. The shortage of energy, and the ever-increasing upward spiral of heating fuel costs, are responsible for a continuing increase in the demand for woodland.

Does anyone imagine that the cost of energy will ever stop rising, let alone level off, or actually decrease? Here is a headline from the December 27, 1981 issue of the *St. Louis Post-Dispatch*:

$1,000 Annual Gas Bill by '85 is Forecast

As it turned out—and you know this was true if you had gas heat at the time—that forecast was probably conservative. It projected average annual increases in gas prices of 16% for 1982 through 1985, even though the average annual increase was 29% for the previous three years.

Well, 1982 was not a good year for gas prices. The increase in prices for that year was more like 30%. Suppose the average annual increase is 29%, just like during the 1979-1981 period. Then your average annual gas bill in 1985 will be $1,379!

If 1982 was any indication, this projection is not only possible, but likely. Are you prepared for heating bills like that? If you own some woodland, you will be!

Not only that, but if you own some woodland soon, it is very likely that many people will want to buy it from you—and you will profit handsomely.

While the specific figures cited here come from a particular period, the underlying forces remain unchanged. Energy costs have continued to rise in cycles, supply disruptions recur, and demand for alternative and local energy sources consistently returns. For this reason, woodland retains a unique value—not only as land, but as a practical resource that responds to long-term economic pressure.

CHAPTER 6

INFLATION

It's Here To Stay!

What is inflation? What causes it? How can you avoid its painful effects? These are all questions that economists and social scientists have been trying to answer for decades, centuries even. Since they don't often agree on the answers, I cannot supply you with any infallible wisdom. I can, however, come closer to answering the first question for you than the others. For the others, I will give you both sides of the story, so to speak, and let you make up your own mind. Part of the problem with trying to come up with answers to these questions is that there are also political versions of each answer.

The supposed cure for inflation often requires policies which are painful to one group or another. Therefore, there is always a lot of propaganda floating around as a result of one or the other trying to gain or retain power and this accounts for a large measure of confusion surrounding these questions.

Still, many people manage to insulate themselves from the effects of inflation—and some even profit handsomely from it. My hope is to help you learn to insulate yourself and your family—and hopefully even to profit from inflation.

Inflation is money becoming less valuable. This year $3.50 may buy, say, one gallon of gas; next year that same gallon might cost $4.25. There are two ways of looking at this, and they both mean the same thing. Obviously, the gas got more expensive by 30% during the year. Or you could say that your dollar got less valuable by 30%. Either way, you could buy less with a dollar after a year of inflation.

What other things increase in price like that during inflation? The answer is nearly everything. Certainly everything that it takes to live—things people must have and, therefore, are forced to buy regardless of the price: food, housing, clothes, gasoline, cars. And, oh yes, land.

Why does a new car cost more than $45,000 today when the very same car cost only $2,200 in 1957? There is no more labor in today's car (probably a lot less). The only answer is that dollars are a whole lot cheaper today—in other words, there are a whole lot more of them.

Everyone knows that when there's a very large supply of something, it will be cheap. If, in a given year, there is a very good harvest, and consequently a very large supply of, say, apples, then apples will be cheap. If you were trying to trade apples for that car, you would have to come up with a larger number than usual. It's the same with money: it will become cheaper and buy less when there is a large supply of it.

And just who supplies the money? Well, the government does, that's who. They print it—and for many reasons they often print more and more of it than they should. They do that in order to spend more of it for politically popular projects; if it's popular with a large segment of the people, and politicians can get elected by promising it, then the money will be found to pay for it, and if it can't be found, then it can be printed.

What things will maintain their value during inflation? Well, anything that cannot be supplied in excess—like land. The government cannot print that! In fact, nothing can alter the ever-dwindling supply of good land. You do not even need to worry about a "good harvest" temporarily depressing the prices of land, as you do for most commodities.

And right here you are beginning to get the idea of what this book is all about!

CAN INFLATION BE STOPPED?

It's very unlikely. It can be slowed down or even reduced for short periods of time, but it seems impossible to stop permanently. This has been true for all governments, democratic or imperial, throughout all recorded history.

The Emperor Diocletian of ancient Rome was responsible for one of the earliest recorded examples of uncontrollable inflation in the years 302 to around 325 A.D. He caused it in exactly the same way that today's governments sometimes do: by debasing the money. In order to finance large scale (and popular) military operations in the far reaches of the Empire, Diocletian found that he could mint more gold coins by simply adding zinc or lead to the mixture. At first, only a few percent base metal was added, but as more and more money was needed to finance the Emperor's projects, and no more gold was received through taxation, the silver and gold coins of Rome began to contain less and less precious metal—until finally they were all bronze.

Of course, most merchants and other producers of goods knew that the more recent coins were worth less, so they charged ever higher prices for their goods and services. Finally, in some prosperous colonies, people refused to accept Roman coins at all; and in one, Britain, many merchants actually counterfeited the Roman coins, putting the true amount of precious metal in so that commerce and trade could continue.

Well, that's inflation: single digit when only a small amount of base metal was added; double digit when more than 10% was mixed in; and "raging" when people began to stop accepting the debased coins. People with debased money sought to quickly get rid of it by buying something—anything—that would hold its value. These purchases were most often of real property: land or houses or of the precious metals, such as gold or silver.

There have been other notable examples of inflation gone wild:

- Germany during the years surrounding World War I, when a wheelbarrow load of paper money was necessary to buy even a dozen eggs.
- England and Western Europe in 1972 through 1976.
- Our own double digit inflation in 1976 to 1980.

All of these have resulted from the same practice: debasing the money in one way or another.

There have been periods of relative stability of paper money now and then. England before and during the time of Queen Victoria is one example, and our own country up until 1932 is another. Both of these countries printed paper money, but by law the paper was redeemable in gold and silver. Note that such laws force administrations to print only so much paper money as they have precious metal for backing. We abandoned the gold standard in the early 1930s for our own people, and finally in the early 1970s it was abandoned altogether when the last gold backing was removed for foreign holders of dollars.

The debasement of our money which commenced in the 1930s was gradual. For a long time dollars had been exchangeable for gold at the rate of $20 per troy ounce of precious metal; then later, the rate became $35, then briefly $45, and finally not at all. Just like Diocletian, our postwar administrations have found it necessary to remove the precious metal backing so that they could print ever more paper money.

And the effects have been identical. After 1972, the price of gold soared to historic highs: around $850 per ounce! That was caused by people with paper money buying the real stuff in order to preserve the value of their holdings. Just like those merchants in ancient Britain seeking honest gold coinage, modern people respond the same way to inflation.

But gold is not the best protection against inflation for the average person—not today and probably not in ancient times either. By now you can guess what I will recommend as an effective store of value for you.

THE RETURN OF DOUBLE DIGIT INFLATION? YOU CAN COUNT ON IT!

Why? What will cause another round of rapidly upward spiraling prices? If the government wants to spend money (our money!) that it doesn't have, it has only two alternatives:

- it can print more money, as we've been discussing; or
- it can borrow the required money from the people.

Now we know what printing more money does—the same thing it did for Diocletian. Actually, it is this course—printing—that is favored by many administrations.

But what about borrowing? This is the remedy most favored by many other administrations and politicians. It has equally bad effects and, as we shall show below, it only postpones the return of inflation for the time being. There is also good economic evidence that when inflation does finally return, it does so with a vengeance.

In the meantime, heavy borrowing by the government forces up interest rates. We all know about that! It means that we pay 18% to 29% on revolving credit card charge accounts, and sharply higher interest rates on home mortgages—and maybe the same on an automobile loan. We cannot afford those high monthly payments, so we don't buy a new home and we fix up the old car.

The result of all this is a very sick economy with many people out of work and many businesses in deep trouble or going broke. Hardest hit are small businesses which must have credit at low interest in order to operate. What's happening is that government is borrowing—at high interest—a very large portion of all the available money, leaving too little behind to finance private business operations.

Because many people are being laid off, or are worried about it, they don't spend much. They try to save what they can for a rainy day that might just come sometime soon. So when prices do stop rising so rapidly and inflation seems to stop increasing, the current administration proclaims a "victory," and assures us that inflation is "under control." But the pain is so great that the people will likely not tolerate that administration's economic policies indefinitely.

The housing and auto industries will demand that Congress "do something about high interest rates," and labor will demand that they "do something about high unemployment." No government can resist that kind of pressure for long. A new administration can be voted in at the next election! Then it might print more money to finance the deficits created by overspending—and off we go into the wild blue yonder, once again on the way to double digit inflation.

Of course, the government could avoid printing money and borrowing. But neither side of the political aisle like to do that because the only alternative then is to cut spending and balance the budget. As we have seen, that seems impossible for either the right- or left-wingers to do. It means that they must forego their favorite projects—something that has proven beyond the grasp of nearly all rulers, whether democratic or totalitarian.

So, I predict the return of very high inflation fairly soon. And I'm not alone. Many reputable economists are making the very same predictions.

AND SPEAKING OF REPUTABLE ECONOMISTS . . .

They seem to group around two main explanations for the causes of inflation. I'll repeat them here for you in capsule form. You can take your pick of them, though it doesn't matter which you pick because they both lead to the same conclusion: more—and higher—inflation. The only question is when.

The first argument is the so-called "cost of energy" theory. Everything that is manufactured requires energy to make, and if the cost of energy is much higher, the cost of the items produced with it will also be higher.

There may be some truth in this idea. If so, the inescapable projection is for higher inflation. Gasoline prices have moderated somewhat recently, but everything else you can burn is higher. Natural gas, up the average of 30% per year for the last three years, is projected to increase by similar amounts for the next three (and probably more after that)! Heating oil? The same story and no end of increases in sight.

Hey! How about Firewood? It's also true: up and up. See the next Section for more on this and how you can profit from high energy costs.

The second theory is that inflation is all the fault of the government—that it is always caused by the misguided policies of the previous people in power. The misguided policies are large deficits in the federal budget, along with low interest rates.

As we've seen, that can only be done by printing money. So do you suppose that the conservatives will conquer inflation with balanced budgets? Not a chance, because then they would have to give up their pet spending programs.

Just read the current newspapers! The projected deficits are measured in the hundreds of billions of dollars—and there's no end in sight. Even the conservatives admit that there will be "very large" deficits.

So how is all this red ink to be paid? By printing money—how else? If not just now, then soon.

As we have shown, no government can sustain the prolonged pain of doing anything else for very long. So when they begin printing money in excess again, we shall see high inflation return.

AND THE MORAL OF THE STORY IS: BUY LAND!

Land will increase in value faster than the inflation rate. It always has. Even since Roman times.

Gold and silver, or stocks in the securities markets, might also be good, except that they often decrease in price before increasing in the long run. That is, they go up and down. Believe me, you don't want to be riding with them on the way down! I've been on that ride a few times myself.

But land only goes up—or, at worst, it stays constant in value for a time. And, as we shall see in the coming chapters, country land has many advantages over all other real estate investments during times of high inflation.

CHAPTER 7

A MONEY-MAKING BUSINESS IN YOUR SPARE TIME!

Here It Is! This Is What I Promised You!

All through this book you will be learning how to choose country land for maximum gain in value over a three- to four-year period on a minimal investment of your own money—even no investment at all (see Chapter 16)!

You will also learn how to enjoy that land—doing every weekend (or whenever you want) what many other people regularly pay lots of money to do. And, I'm passing on to you many tips on how to improve the quality of your life as well.

But that's only half the story! The other half is that you can turn any piece of country woodland into your own, highly profitable, weekend business.

The income from this home-operated business can easily pay off your purchase of the woodland with loads of money to spare. Believe it! Three years from now, you and your family will be well on your way to real wealth and you will thank your lucky stars that you had the courage and good sense to start this business today.

How can this be? How is it possible to make money two ways?

At the bottom of it is the basic value of an acre of woodland. Here's what I'm talking about.

A LIVING SOLAR COLLECTOR FOR A FEW BUCKS!

That's what a tree is, and a thing of great beauty as well, and there can be as many as 1,000 of them on a typical acre of woodland! And, you can buy that acre of woodland for as low as a few hundred dollars. Well now! That works out to almost nothing per tree—and that has to be the bargain of the century!

You want land that also meets our targets for doubling in value in three to four years. So, let's say $2,200 is typical for the type of land we are looking for. And it is a great bargain when you compare it to anything else $2,200 will buy for you, such as fixing your air conditioner, tuning up your imported sports car, life insurance for six months, a new suit of clothes (and not very good quality clothes at that), and a host of other conveniences and frivolities.

Hey! How about your heating bill for just one winter month? In many cases, one cord of wood will heat a typical small home for about a month. And, with proper woodland management, you can often take roughly one cord of wood per year from one acre of woodland on a renewable basis.

A single mature hardwood tree may yield a substantial portion of a cord of wood[1], and the annual growth of an acre of healthy woodland can replace that harvested volume over time.

So, theoretically, with your one-time investment of $2,200, you could secure a month's heat for your home year after year, for as long as you own the land. That's the kind of basic value we're talking about.

YOUR OWN WEEKEND WINTER BUSINESS, WHICH CAN GROSS $24,000+ PER YEAR

Now, suppose you cut down one of your living solar collectors and convert it into firewood. What would it be worth? If you live in or near a large city, you are in luck. A cord of firewood commonly sells for anywhere from $300 to $600, depending on location and season. Sound good? Not really. That's not where the real money is made.

1 A cord of wood is a stack cut and split in 2-foot lengths. The stack measures 4 ft. × 4 ft. × 8 ft.

You don't sell firewood to homeowners by the cord. Plenty of people do that and do reasonably well, but that isn't the most profitable approach. Instead, you sell firewood by the bundle, and you sell it to supermarkets, convenience stores, and all-night grocery and drug stores.

Firewood in drug stores? Absolutely. Go into almost any convenience store in the winter and look at what they sell for fireplaces and wood stoves. You've seen them before—manufactured fire logs. Look at the price. They sell for $4.50 to $6.00 each, and each one burns about as long as a good hardwood fire log from a bundled stack of real wood.

From the wood harvested from an acre of managed woodland, you can produce hundreds of individual firewood pieces, depending on species and how they are cut. When bundled and sold at retail through stores, the value of that same wood rises dramatically. Of course, you sell those bundles to the stores at a discount. Suppose you give them roughly half the retail price.

Even with that allowance, you can reasonably expect to process two to four cords per weekend. At just two cords per weekend, you are looking at a gross monthly income in the range of roughly $1,500 to $3,000, depending on pricing and volume. This woodheat business can operate for four to five months each year in most regions—and in the Northern States, often six or seven months.

I don't have to spell out what that kind of additional income can mean in terms of improving the quality of your life.

THIS WOODHEAT BUSINESS IS RECESSION PROOF

That's the best part. Energy costs in general—and heating costs in particular—have repeatedly risen faster than the general inflation rate, with sharp spikes occurring during periods of supply disruption and market stress. Natural gas pricing has undergone major changes over the years, and these shifts continue to place upward pressure on all heating costs.

With your woodheat business, you are positioned to benefit directly from each new cycle of higher energy prices. At the same time, you will be improving the quality and value of your woodland. Most country woodland has gone untended for long periods of time, and careful thinning improves both the growth and appearance of what remains.

HOW MUCH WOODLAND DO YOU NEED TO GET STARTED?

You are going to be moving some 32 cords of wood per year. If you wish to make it a completely renewable operation, where nature will replace every cord of wood you remove with natural growth, you will need about 32 acres. With proper thinning and good hardwood growth, however, you can often operate successfully on as little as ten acres. I do recommend thinning, because it improves the woodland and increases the value of your land. And anyone can afford to buy ten acres of land!

In the following chapters of this book, I will show you how to acquire that ten acres, and much more. You will also learn how to choose it for maximum capital gain—even how to buy it with no money, but for now you need to know what to look for in order to make your firewood business most successful.

That's fairly easy: Look for hardwoods.

- Hickory is best, because it is the most fragrant smelling, and it burns long with high heat output.
- Oak is the next best, and that is fortunate because it is one of the most common hardwoods growing in the United States.
- Maple, ash, and sweet gum are all fine as well.
- Avoid pine. It provides high heat, but burns too rapidly.

In addition to paying attention to the type of wood, you need also to seek good access. Road frontage is important, and you will also find it very convenient to have a single-lane path or trail through your land.

Look also for land which is not too rugged. You need a vehicle near where you will be cutting, so stay away from property that has deep ravines or is strewn with large rocks or other barriers.

Finally, if you are searching for property in the spring, look for the flowers.

The flowers?

YES! IN THE SPRING YOU CAN SELL WILD FLOWERS AND DECORATIVE TREES

You wouldn't believe the demand for wild flowers and decorative trees. In the spring, they can be sold in substantial quantities in supermarket parking lots and similar high-traffic locations for around $25 to $50 each, depending on size and local demand.

What kinds of wild flowers grow in your area? Here are some that are very popular and may be obtained by careful digging at your country place (subject to local conservation and harvesting regulations):

- Lily of the Valley
- Virginia Bluebells
- Lady's Slipper
- Shooting Star
- Dog Tooth Violet
- Jack-in-the-Pulpit
- Dutchman's Breeches
- Tradescantia
- Many varieties of ferns
- Wild Roses

I leave it to you to check the prices of these at your neighborhood nursery or in your favorite seed catalogue, if you can find them at all. All you need to cash in on this Spring and Summer business is a good book of wild flowers and native trees for your area.[2]

Do I need to estimate for you how much you can make? It will depend on location and other factors. A large farmer's market is always a good location if there is one in your area. I'm sure you can develop detailed plans and profit projections for this business.

Well, there you have it! I've given you many reasons for buying or investing in country land. And here I've shown you how to make very nice profits from two home-operated businesses that you can start with as little as ten acres of country woodland. I predict that within only three to four years (that's the most desirable "hold time" for doubling your money on well-chosen property) you will be hiring people to operate your firewood and flower businesses and telling your present boss to go fly a kite!

2 Contact your state or local environmental authorities to make sure there are no laws against flower harvesting on your property.

CHAPTER 8

ESTIMATING VALUE

Constant Practice and Up-to-Date Information Will Improve Your Skills

Accurate appraisal of country land is an art that is improved with experience. This is because many aspects, which are difficult to measure or quantify, play important roles in the attractiveness (or lack thereof) of a particular piece of property.

Nevertheless, anyone willing to devote some time and effort to the practice of estimating values can gain a reasonably good feel for the worth of land in a fairly short period. This will require more than just a couple of weekends out in the car, but a competent enough skill level can be obtained in, say, a few months.

Before we bought our first property, my wife and I spent six months looking and pricing. We were wasting quite a bit of time, though, because we didn't know exactly what to look for or how to evaluate the attractions and/or flaws in property.

In this chapter I will show you exactly what to look for and what to avoid. After some practice, your ability to appraise a parcel will almost become second nature. The key word here is "practice."

It is important to realize that an "eye for value" is indeed a continuously developing talent. My wife and I make it a point to drive out into the country every few weekends even when we are not interested in buying at that particular time. We try to guess the value of a few nice farms or other country properties, and we often take some notes and obtain the names of the owners. Later on in the week we call the owners to ask if they would be interested in selling and, if so, what they think their land is worth. Even if they are not in the mood to sell, they will often talk about value: "Why just last year the old Hickerson place just up the road a piece went for $780 an acre!"

You will need to check out the "old Hickerson place" on your next trip for all aspects which might increase or decrease its value. Later on in this chapter we will discuss those particular factors that affect the value of country land.

We have found that most country people will welcome phone calls inquiring about the value of their land and if they have ever considered selling. Remember, they should be approached courteously, as should all your business contacts. A note of praise for the particular beauty or value of the land in their local region is always a good conversation opener—and almost always, gratefully received.

You should always read the "Acreage, Land, and Farms for Sale" listings in your weekend paper. Pay particular attention to location (see the next chapter!) and asking price if it is listed. Don't hesitate to phone up the owner or real estate listing agent to ask the price and other questions pertaining to value. You can learn a lot without it costing you anything by frequently using the phone. Make extensive notes from your phone calls and follow-up the calls with visits to those properties you asked about during your next jaunt out. Remember, frequent practice will improve your skill.

ASPECTS THAT INCREASE THE VALUE OF COUNTRY LAND

Within commuting distance of a large city, the value of land is determined in large measure by the distance out and the direction out from the city center. We will discuss these two aspects in much greater detail in Chapters 9 and 11.

The two other major factors which influence value are the road accessibility and the ease and desirability of subdividing. Here is a bit of wisdom, called the subdivider's rule:

The sum of the parts is worth more than the whole!

This is unlike the rules of geometry or physics. What the subdivider's rule means is that, generally speaking, land in smaller parcels sells for more dollars per acre than land in much larger tracts. For example, if you bought 200 acres for $2,500 per acre and then divided it into two equal parts, you might expect to reasonably obtain about 25% more or $3,125 per acre. Divide down by four—or into 50 acre parcels—and ask 50% over your purchase price, or $3,750 per acre.[1]

Dividing further into 25-acre units would entitle you to around $5,000 or 100% over your purchase price. You can see that the percentage markup increases rapidly as the final parcels become smaller. There are many people who make large amounts of money simply by buying and subsequently dividing down, then reselling without ever waiting for time and inflation to work their wondrous (or barbarous, depending on your point of view) magic.

Here are some characteristics or aspects of particular parcels which increase their value:

1. **Access.** Lengthy frontage on a paved road is desirable. A corner property with additional road frontage on one other or two other sides is even better. Generally, the more road frontage, the more valuable.
2. **Water.** Frontage on a river, stream, or lake with good recreational opportunities, such as fishing, canoeing, water skiing, is very desirable. On large parcels, all season springs, streams, and lake sites add greatly to the value.
3. **Shape and topography.** A regular shape such as a rectangle is easier to subdivide. The topography

1 Actual premiums vary widely by market conditions, access, zoning, and demand, but the general relationship between parcel size and per-acre price remains consistent.

should be gently rolling with all parts of the parcel usable.

4. **Views.** High ground with sweeping, scenic views has recently been in strong demand. To many people, a restful, peaceful view is worth more and works much better than a session with a psychiatrist.
5. **Wildlife.** Abundant deer, turkeys, quail, and the like are the fond dream of every hunter, animal photographer, or just plain nature lover. If your land borders a national forest or park, your wildlife is more likely to remain indefinitely and you don't have to be worried about being eventually surrounded by development. Also, remember that we are out to improve the quality of your own life as well. You can hunt and put game food on your family's table while your land appreciates in value. This is just another way in which you can make your own pleasure pay for itself many, many times over.
6. **Income Potential.** Never neglect this item! A perfectly ordinary piece of land that can be made to produce some income (even small income) will immediately increase in value. Can you put up a fence and lease the pasture to a neighbor? Is there an old house that could be rented after a few minor repairs? Is there saleable timber or firewood? Or you might discover a grove of black walnut trees, which, when mature, sometimes sell for many thousands of dollars each!

The above list is by no means complete. I'm certain that you can add many items and, as you gain experience, many other ways to increase the value of your property will occur to you.

AND SOME WHICH DECREASE IT. TRAPS TO AVOID!

Look carefully for any of the following defects in any parcel which you might otherwise be thinking about buying. Scrutinize carefully! Most especially if you are buying from real estate agents representing the seller. Many real estate agents won't point these out to you and, in fact, will likely try to disguise them. If they actively attempt to disguise any unfavorable feature, especially in a written description of the land, they may be exposing themselves to legal liability. To get out of the deal (even after closing or after you've put money down), you may have legal grounds to challenge the transaction for misrepresentation. They will cheerfully and quickly refund your money, as the saying goes, even if they are not actually guilty or if it's questionable. They hope to avoid at all costs the bad publicity that goes with this accusation.

Here are some other risks to avoid.

1. **Access Again.** If the only access is by easement over someone else's road or, worse yet, by nondeeded "agreement," you are in for endless arguments ("Whose turn is it to gravel the road this winter? Mine?! But, I only come out here in the summer and you live here all year around!") and possibly some expensive legal problems.
2. **And Water Also.** If there is none, and a test well comes up dry, you are in trouble! Wells often cost many thousands of dollars. Some people insert conditional clauses into their sale contracts which guarantee escape if a well turns up dry. Look carefully also for any sign of flooding (that's the other side of the coin!) if there is a river or stream adjoining or passing through the property.
3. **Easements and Rights.** These are recorded in the deed and should always be checked. A power line overhead or a gas pipeline below will show up as an

easement on the deed. Mineral rights are especially troublesome. My advice is absolutely don't buy it if the mineral rights have been previously sold off—even if they were sold off in 1880 to a mining company that doesn't even exist today. Somewhere, somebody or his heirs has that right! Also, look out for agricultural rights. Sometimes farmers will purchase the right to farm a particular piece of land for a specific length of time or for an indefinite time, and this right will appear in the deed.

4. **Scrubby Trees and Brush.** Land which was timbered off 15 to 20 years ago, and untended since, shows overcrowded trees and brush today. The trees will all have about the same diameter— around 6 to 8 inches at the base of the trunks. Such growth is not worth much, even for firewood. In addition, and sometimes this is even a worse problem, the top soil may have been allowed to erode severely after the trees were originally removed.

5. **Percolation.** This is a measure of how fast water sinks into the ground after having been poured into a standard size hole. Most counties have percolation test requirements which must be met before they will issue a building permit. Land which does not percolate water rapidly enough cannot sustain a septic tank.

6. **Irregular Shape and/or Rugged Topography.** A parcel that is 200 feet wide by three miles long (railroad land!) is difficult, if not impossible, to sell for anything but small-time gardening. Also, beware of too rugged or rocky terrain. When you divide down, you will need to build a road to access the back plots, and road building is much more expensive if the rock must be blasted. This also applies to some home

building as well, since rock blasting may be necessary to excavate the basements.

Again, this list is certainly not complete. You can add to it as you gain experience. For any particular parcel , there may be some defects which are not on any list—yours or mine. The best test is to think through exactly what possibilities the land offers—subdivision with road building, housing, etc.—and see if you encounter any defects along the way. Always walk over every foot of a piece before you consider buying.[2]

COMPARABLES

A parcel of land, like anything else in this world, is worth exactly what someone is willing to pay for it—no more and no less. That must be somebody's law, but I haven't a clue whose. If a particular property has recently been sold for $8,500 per acre to someone, then it is safe to assume that a similar piece in the same or similar location is also worth $8,500 per acre because, it is assumed, someone else will be found who is willing to pay as much. Such a similar piece is called a **comparable.**

Comparable pricing is widely used in home sales, where it is relatively easy to find several comparables in a given neighborhood. Most houses in a neighborhood are similar, having been built at around the same time to be sold in a somewhat narrow price range. With country land, it is much more difficult to find good comparables because no two parcels are exactly alike or even very similar. Every one is unique.

That makes trading country land interesting and challenging—and pricing is difficult. Also, country land does not turn over as rapidly as homes in a neighborhood do, so you might find a perfectly good comparable that sold five years ago. In that case you can still use the comparable, but you

2 We always do this twice. A second time a few weeks after we've first gone over it, and had time to think about it and jot down any questions.

must calculate its current price from your knowledge of the rate at which prices have been rising in that area.

For example, suppose your comparable sold for $3,500 per acre five years ago and land prices have been rising at rates of 12% to 18% per year in a time of increasing inflation. You assume that the price increase went at the 12% rate for the first three years and at the 18% rate during the last two years. The five years of growth in prices up to the present time would look like this[3]:

Sale price (original)	$3,500 per acre	
First year	$ 3,920	($3,500 x 1.12)
Second year	$ 4,390	($3,920 x 1.12)
Third year	$ 4,920	($4,390 x 1.12)
Fourth year	$ 5,800	($4,920 x 1.18)
Fifth year	$ 6,850	($5,800 x 1.18)

So, that comparable which sold for $3,500 five years ago, would be worth $6,850 if it were on the market today. You can bet that the property you are interested in, which is similar to the comparable, is worth very close to $6,850 today.

In trying to come up with good comparable prices, you may have to make other adjustments as well. Suppose the property you are interested in has good road frontage on two sides, but the comparable you've managed to locate has it on only one side. An extra side of road frontage is worth 15% to 25% more on the total value depending on how long the second frontage is.

You should discount the value of land in comparison to a good comparable if any portions of it are unusable for any reason. For example, suppose the comparable is worth $5,500 per acre, but the land you are trying to price is only four-fifths usable. Maybe it is 50 acres total, but 10 acres flood periodi-

3 This example illustrates the method, not a prediction of future rates.

cally or are too steep and rugged to be of use. Then that land is only worth $4,400 per acre ($5,500 x 4/5).

Distance from an attraction, such as an urban center or recreation area, also plays a role in finding comparable prices. If your land is nearer, you must increase the price accordingly. In Chapter 11, I will show you exactly how to handle these problems using a graphical analysis called "extrapolation."

FINDING OUT THE PRICE

All this leaves you with exactly one problem: how to find out what price a particular parcel sold for when you know that it was sold. In some states this is not as easy as it might seem.

The deed is a matter of public record, so you can go to the office of the Recorder of Deeds and look it up, but it might say something like "for $10 and other valuable consideration . . ."[4]

However, there may still be a way out. Look on the deed for a tax stamp; if there is one, note down the amount of tax paid. Then ask the county tax collector for the deed transfer tax rate. He or she might say something like "20¢ per $100," so if the sale price was $200,000 (that is, $2,000 units of $100), then the tax would have been $2,000 × .20 = $400 and that's what the tax stamp would show.

It doesn't always work like that because some counties don't have a deed transfer tax.

Of course, other states require the deeds to show the exact and true sale price—and some even require that this information be published in the county newspaper as a matter of public record.

4 See Chapter 15 for more details on this.

CHAPTER 9

LOCATION, LOCATION, LOCATION

How To Find The Next Gold Mine

"Three things are important in real estate investments," goes an old saying in the trade, "and they are: location, location, and location."

This adage is most often applied to home sales where the whole character of a neighborhood—schools, shopping centers, architecture, etc.—determines its desirability. A neighborhood is a location. The same is true of country land. Some areas are simply less desirable than others. Sometimes the reasons are obvious:

- the land is boring and flat
- the land was timbered off
- the land was allowed to erode
- the land is now grown up in scrub
- the land may be near a factory that pollutes the air

We know a perfectly beautiful region lying in the crook of a scenic and popular river with everything going for it—views, gently rolling hills, nice mix of mature forest and meadowland, easy access to a popular urban area, etc.

There's only one trouble: it's near a coal-burning power plant with very tall smoke stacks, which can be seen from nearly every location in the surrounding countryside. This is a kind of visual pollution that is no less objectionable than the fumes and gases given off. Location again! If this area were located away from the power plant, it would be worth twice to three times what it now sells for.

NEAR AN URBAN CENTER

Even those of you who wish to purchase far from urban centers should pay attention to location because it will greatly affect future increases in the value of your land. Some areas, even far from cities, are much more desirable than others. In Chapter 12, I outline the principles of trading in vacation land for fun and large profit. Here we are going to look at some factors which make country land, which is adjacent to an urban center, desirable and profitable.

Most of us are tied to city jobs, either because we have to work to support ourselves and our families or because we enjoy working and are stimulated by the opportunities that city living affords us. If this is the case with you, you will wish to begin your land investment and acquisition program closer in.

That's actually very fortunate because the closer to an urban center a particular parcel is, the more rapidly it appreciates in value compared to the properties much farther out. This has always been true.

While country land in general is, and has always been, the best long-term investment that anyone can buy, an even better investment has been that country land on the fringes of a rapidly growing urban area.[1]

We have found that about an hour's driving time from your home is the practical limit. Anything more distant is just too much trouble to visit very often. This is a very important point because you will be doing many things to derive income from your land and to improve it. You're going to be cutting wood, transplanting and selling wild flowers, picnicking, thinning, and reforesting, etc.[2]

---

1 And remember! You will want to enjoy your land while waiting for it to appreciate in value, so it should be reasonably close to where you live and work.

2 Actually, this sort of list is limited only by your own imagination. For example, we have recently fenced some property we own and we plan to put some calves out in a barter arrangement with a country neighbor. Next year, we will have a much better and less expensive supply of beef than we have ever had—and we will have greatly increased the value of our property in the bargain.

So your land needs to be near enough that you can easily visit it regularly, at least in the spring and summer. The things you will be doing will be enjoyable, will serve to provide income, will improve the quality of your life, and will add to your profits by increasing the value of your land.

Now you can draw a circle on your road map, with the center at your home and with a radius that corresponds to about an hour's drive from home. That will be a lot of land to start looking at!

The next question, of course, is where to look inside that circle? In answer to that question, John Jacob Astor, a department store tycoon who actually made his largest fortune in Manhattan Island real estate (long after the Indians had sold it for a handful of beads!), is reported to have said, "Buy on the fringe and wait."

That's good advice, if you can determine where future development is going to happen so that you can buy on the "fringe" of that expansion.

So how do you do that? The answer is that it's always true that expansion and development—and the rapidly rising prices that go along with that activity—seem to happen along certain preferred directions out from an urban center. And the momentum of this growth builds up over the years and cannot be changed rapidly. Therefore, if you can determine the directions of growth in the past, it is a near certainty that there will be continued, rapid growth in the same direction for a long time into the future.

All you need to do to grow rich is simply invest in country land out in front of the direction of growth.

THE PLAT BOOK

There are many reasons for growth moving along certain preferred directions. Sometimes development is forced toward or away from a certain place by geological barriers, such as rivers or mountain ranges.

In other directions, the causes are not always obvious. Growth may follow along a certain path simply because "everybody's buying out there" or "that's where the action is." In other words, that particular direction has, for reasons unknown, become fashionable.

We don't need to know the causes; we only need to know the directions of preferred growth. The first step in discovering these directions is to obtain plat books, or, as they are sometimes called, land atlases, for all the counties surrounding your urban area.

Plat books are very large-scale maps of a county that show the boundaries of each farm or other large property, along with the names of the owners. As we shall see later, knowing the names of the owners can be invaluable information. For our present purpose, however, the books will show us all the land divisions and their sizes in the countryside surrounding the city.

The county plat book can usually be obtained from the Office of the Recorder of Deeds or from the County Clerk's Office in the county seat. If, for some reason, you cannot go to the county seat, or if the office is out of stock, you can order a plat book from a commercial publisher such as Farm and Home Publishers, which maintains plat books for most counties in the country. Their website is: *https://www.farmandhomepublishers.com.*

It is better to obtain the book from the county seat if at all possible, since the taxpayers of the county subsidize the cost in part.

Today, much of the information once found only in printed plat books is also available online. Most counties now maintain **GIS (Geographic Information System)** mapping websites that show parcel boundaries, acreage, road frontage, zoning classifications, and—often—the names of current owners. These systems allow you to zoom from a county-wide view down to individual parcels, making it easy to observe patterns of subdivision and growth over time.

County GIS maps are typically found by searching online for the county name followed by "GIS" or "parcel map." Many are free to use, although the depth of available information varies by county. Some systems show ownership and parcel history clearly; others provide only boundary and zoning data.

Online mapping tools have several advantages. They are current, searchable, and allow rapid comparison across wide areas. They also make it easy to overlay roads, waterways, flood zones, and other features that influence land value.

However, printed plat books still have value. They present the entire county in a consistent, uncluttered format and make long-term development patterns easier to see at a glance. For this reason, many experienced land investors use both: online tools for detailed research and verification, and plat books for spotting broad trends and preferred directions of growth.

The first thing you will notice when leafing through your plat book is that the closer into the city you look, the smaller and smaller are the individual plots of owned land. Conversely, the farther out you look, the larger become the divisions, until finally they are all large working farms. This shows very clearly that land division and resale—growth and development in other words—has been going on for many years. And this development will continue into the indefinite future.

People who buy land in front of the growth will usually earn a lot of money. The plat book also shows quite clearly the preferred directions of this growth. The most obvious of these are the directions followed by the major highways out from the city.

The large number of small tracts within easy access of good roads shows that for many years city people, or people who must work in the city and commute, have been buying land "on the fringe" of development. Many of these people are investors like yourself, who are in the process of becoming wealthy landowners.

Others, in fact the great majority, are simply people who want to own some land. They are people who just want to cut wood or picnic on their land, and who often hope to someday build a retirement home out there. Believe it! There are thousands of such people living in every city, each with some land and a desire to own more.

And there are hundreds of thousands with as-yet-unfulfilled desires to own their first piece. You will always be able to find a buyer for your land when you are ready to sell, and you should make a handsome profit if you closely follow the system presented in this book.

You will no doubt notice other directions which are developing because of recreational opportunities or other attractions. Look in the vicinity of, and along the directions toward, some of the following:

1. **Scenic lakes or rivers** which offer fishing and water sports.
2. **Higher ground** which offers good access along the sweeping views.
3. **Large public recreational areas** such as parks or national forests.
4. **Private parks** such as amusement or theme parks.
5. **Craft villages.** These are really hot right now! Everybody seems to want land nearby, or to build in or near these charming small towns.
6. **Industrial parks** for light manufacturing—so-called "clean" factories. There is a trend toward building these well out from cities, but not too far away from

places where they can obtain the services necessary to their operations.

These are only a few of the magnets which cause growth in certain preferred directions out from a city. I'm sure you can supply a number of others. But, even if the causes for directional growth are unknown, you can easily discover the good locations with your plat book.

CHAPTER 10

BARGAIN HUNTING

More Fun Than The Flea Market And Much More Profitable

Everyone enjoys finding a bargain—and you can learn to enjoy the search for one too. Bargain hunting is one of the most exciting and consistently pleasurable activities you will pursue in the course of buying and selling country land for profit. Every piece of property you look at is potentially a bargain.

In order to be properly called a bargain, my rule of thumb says that you should not have to pay more than around 70% of the current market.

As you begin to sense that your negotiations will be successful, and that you will actually obtain a chosen parcel for a bargain price, a wonderful sense of pride and pleasure begins to flow over you. You know that you are going to make a lot of money! Very few activities in life can compete with this one for the sheer excitement and gratifying sense of personal accomplishment that you will feel.

HOW TO SEARCH FOR A BARGAIN

To find a bargain, you must first be able to recognize one when you see it. This means that, as always, you must have done your homework for the area of your current interest and you must actively keep it up to date.[1]

Then you must always be on the lookout for that "undiscovered paradise." An undiscovered paradise is any property that you know will come into high demand in the moderately near future and that you have reason to believe can be purchased for significantly under the market price. You may

1 Continuously doing the time/distance analysis (see Chapter 11) is the best way to keep your knowledge of values current and up-to-date.

expect to pay a low price for any number of reasons: distress sales, estate closures, bank-owned properties, or simply that the owner doesn't know the value of the land.

You must always be on the lookout for these goodies. Having found a potential bargain, you must then begin negotiating for a bargain price and terms. Remember that you will not actually have obtained a bargain until you have a signed sale contract in your hands.

NEGOTIATING

Successful negotiating techniques are one of the most important aspects of bargain hunting. You will be seeking to convince the seller to agree to your price and terms. This old cliché may seem time-worn and tired, but it is as useful today as it was on that first day some forgotten negotiator uttered it:

Start with a low price—one well under that which you are finally willing to pay. You can always raise your offer, but you can never go down.

You would be surprised how many earnest people neglect this simple beginning ploy, usually because they imagine themselves to be "reasonable" people. Price-and-terms negotiation is no place to be "reasonable." One person's reasonable terms are another's outrage, so be persistent.

You may, and indeed you must, give some ground in the course of negotiations in order to convince the seller that you are willing to "go some distance" to meet his or her asking price and terms, but you must remain firm on the bargain price that your analysis has provided.

The most important characteristic of a good negotiator is patience. That, in combination with persistence, will often result in success.

Having located a prospective bargain, you may approach the owner only to get a firm "no!" in response to your inquiries. Try again a few months later. Owners often change their minds—and your first call may have been just the jog he or she needed to start thinking about selling. This situation most often occurs when dealing with a longtime owner, one who has farmed or lived on the land for years and hasn't ever thought of it as "for sale."

One final point on making offers through real estate agents is important to keep in mind. I mention it here because, surprisingly, many people are unaware of it or neglect it. You can be certain that your friendly agent, who is trying desperately to sell you something, won't point it out to you unless he is forced to. It is simply that in most states, agents are required by law to transmit all offers to the owners they represent. That means that if you insist on making an offer that, according to your intrepid agent, is "ridiculously low," he must write out a sales contract and present it to the owners.

The agent will usually follow his "ridiculously low" characterization of your offer with something like, "I wouldn't insult my client with an offer like that!" Don't listen! He must transmit the contract—no matter what the terms.

It sometimes happens that a seller will accept a "ridiculously low" contract and, when he does, you are in honey and cream.

The thing to remember is that you do not know what is going on inside the seller's head: he may be in distress or he may be just plain tired of that property or whatever. It simply pays (and pays you very well, thank you!) to make bargain offers.

INSIDE AND ADVANCE KNOWLEDGE

You know that something is going to happen that will vastly increase the value of land that you have been studying and that interests you! That's insider and advance knowledge.

Probably more fortunes have been made in real estate in this way than in any other way. Here's a case that actually happened in my family. In 1939 and 1940, my family took some vacations in the Southwest, spending most of their time in Arizona. Desert land at that time could be bought for around 35 to 50 cents per acre.[2]

My father wanted to buy some, because, even though it was useless for anything at the time, he thought (correctly!) that any land at that price had to be a bargain. As it turned out, he did not buy, even though he went a second time to look the following summer.

That land currently is selling for $2,500 to $3,600 per acre! Why? It was irrigated by the government shortly after the war during 1946 to 1955. The few people who had inside knowledge of those irrigation projects made vast fortunes. The government funded that irrigation project with your tax money—and it made some insiders very, very rich. That land became remarkably fertile when water was poured on it. It is now some of the best fruit and vegetable growing land in the country.

Similar things happen, though on a smaller scale, nearly every year in some part of the country—and probably often enough in your state.

Here are some things that, if you can obtain inside and advance knowledge of, will lead you to vast profits:

1. **Imminent changes in zoning to a higher and better use than before.** It helps to be a member of the zoning board, or to be friends with one.
2. **Where a new lake will be built.** Usually by the Corps of Engineers for the government.
3. **Major highway projects.** These always open up more remote areas to recreation and commercial enterprise.
4. **Where a shopping center or industrial park is to**

2 Yes, cents per acre!

be located. Again, you may learn of this first through the zoning board.

5. **Where a major new industrial plant is to be built.** All its employees will need places to live, shop, and send their kids to school.
6. **Industrial development bonds and "enterprise zones."** Nearly every state now suffering from high unemployment and decreasing state revenues due to a recession has plans to stimulate its own economy with devices such as these. Even the federal government is discussing such plans for stimulating the local economy of especially distressed areas. Land in these distressed areas can be had at bargain prices now, but you will need inside knowledge to mark large profits.

BUT THE BEST BARGAIN IS PROPER TIMING!

Anyone who bought a house 12 to 15 years ago can attest to this. That house has increased in value many times over.[3] The reason most people have profited handsomely from their homes is timing. They bought at just the right time just before our recent spate of inflation.

By contrast, those who had to buy their homes more recently have not done well at all. They got in only on the tail end of inflation, just before the last recession.[4]

---

3 But not as greatly as country land, as we've read in Chapter 4!

4 I am convinced that history is again approaching a familiar turning point. Periods of recession tend to tighten cash, expand opportunity, and place quality country land on the market at compelling prices. Inflation has historically proven difficult to restrain for long without severe political cost, and persistent deficits combined with pressure for lower interest rates have often preceded renewed inflationary cycles. Such conditions have repeatedly favored tangible assets, particularly land. Those positioned early have traditionally benefited as capital moves out of paper and into real property. *(Editor's note: written in 2025.)*

CHAPTER 11

TIME/DISTANCE ANALYSIS

How Prices Move With Time and Distance

In this chapter, I will show you how to estimate value based on distance from an urban center or other high demand area, such as a vacation resort or popular retirement village.

In addition to the distance analysis, the price of land anywhere can be recorded over some time period and the future value estimated. This type of analysis is often helpful for visualizing trends.

The time analysis helps improve your timing, and the distance analysis helps improve your estimates of the influence of location on values. I have discussed the importance of location in Chapter 9, and the profit potential augmented by good timing was emphasized in the last chapter.

It is important to realize that these analyses are only guides to future price behavior. No one and no analysis can predict the future with absolute certainty.

In addition, the value of a given property at a particular location and time may depend on a variety of factors, as I have discussed in Chapters 7 and 8. Still, a good picture of the overall trends of price movements in your area, both with distance from an attraction and with time, can be of great value.

DISTANCE FIRST

I use a graphical analysis for making these estimates, and for visualizing the influence of distance on value. The easiest way to show this is by an actual example.

This distance analysis was necessary to answer a very particular question. The question was: *How much is a piece of land worth, if it is located 41 miles out on good roads (e.g., an interstate highway) from a highly developed suburban area adjacent to a large metropolitan center?*

Now this property is easily divisible for building houses on "mini-estates" of 5 to 10 acres each. It is, in fact, surrounded by quality homes already built on similar parcels, on three sides. On the fourth side, it adjoins undeveloped land which is difficult to access. All-in-all, a nearly ideal property.

So how much is it now worth? We shall do a distance analysis at a particular time: Spring 1982.

In order to carry out the analysis, it is necessary to find some similar properties closer in which are currently being offered for sale. We shall need to know their asking prices and from these, or from finding some comparables, we shall need to make estimates of the actual prices for which we could expect them to sell. The minimum number of such similar properties we will need is three.

Of course, the analysis becomes more accurate in its predictions if more "data" (more similar properties) can be found. In this analysis, I will use only three, but you will get the idea, and you can add to the analysis as many additional properties as you can find.

It is important to try to find similar parcels that is, they should be available for the same use, and dividable down to about the same final sizes. Here are our data:

- **Property A.** 15.2 miles out from the same developed suburban area. "Estates" offered in 5- to 10-acre sizes. Many homes are already built. The asking price is $8,600 to $9,500 per acre, depending on size and location within the development. Not quite as good access as the next two, but located in a larger area for housing.
- **Property B.** 20.3 miles out. This is a 20-acre "horse ranch" with a stable already built. Good access, with a private road at its entrance and all along one long

side. After subtracting the price of the stable, the asking price is $4,500 to $4,900 per acre.

- **Property C.** 31.5 miles out. A 33-acre, partly-open, partly-wooded piece with a very nice view. Good access and easily dividable. Located out the same highway as B. Asking price is $3,600 "firm," but it probably could be had for $3,100.
- **Property D.** 41.0 miles out; 25 acres, dividable and with an excellent view. This is the one we are interested in. We need to determine an asking price for this property with the graphical analysis.

Property D happens to belong to my wife and me. We plan to offer it for sale this spring, having owned it for a little over three years. The question is *what is a reasonable asking price?* The graph shown below helps to answer this question.

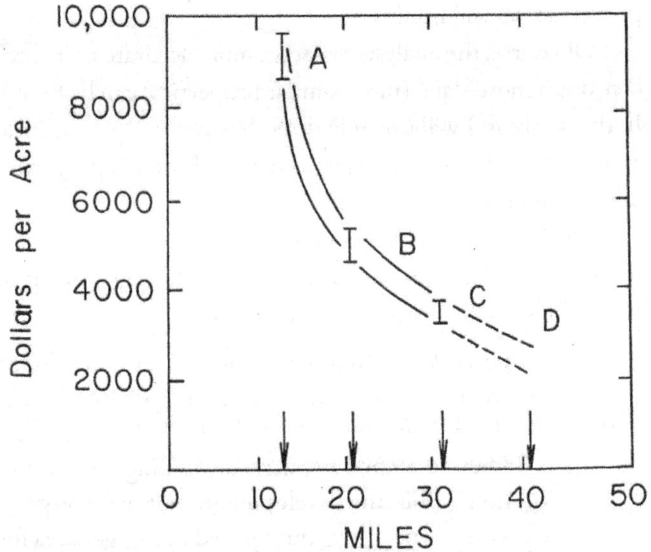

Here's how the analysis was made: Originally, I used graph paper—the kind with one-inch-by-one-inch squares. A five-inch-by-five-inch box works well. The vertical axis represents price per acre, scaled in $2,000 increments: $2,000, $4,000, $6,000, $8,000, and $10,000. The horizontal axis represents distance from the suburban center, with each inch standing for ten miles: 10, 20, 30, and 40 miles.

Today, the exact same analysis can be done more quickly using a spreadsheet or basic charting software such as Excel, Google Sheets, or similar tools. The principle is identical: price per acre on the vertical axis, distance on the horizontal axis. Digital tools simply make the plotting faster and the adjustments easier.

Once the axes are established, locate each comparable property along the distance axis. Properties A, B, C, and D fall at 15.2, 20.3, 31.5, and 41 miles out, respectively.

Now plot the asking prices. For Property A, follow its distance point upward and mark the upper asking price with a small horizontal tick. Then mark the lower asking price just beneath it and draw a short vertical line connecting the two. This vertical segment represents the realistic price range for that property. Repeat the process for Properties B and C.

Next, draw a smooth curve through the upper price ticks for A, B, and C, extending the curve out to the distance of Property D. Do the same with the lower price ticks. Because Property D has no existing price, the extension of these curves estimates its likely value. This process—called extrapolation—is widely used in science, engineering, and market analysis to estimate unknown values from known trends.

From this graph, Property D's estimated price range becomes clear: approximately $2,200 to $2,400 per acre. Based on this analysis, I would offer the property at $2,400 per acre and accept an offer of $2,200.

I originally purchased the land for $800 per acre a little over three years earlier. This result fits squarely within our target of achieving roughly a 300% increase in value over a three-to-four-year period—achieved not by guesswork, but by disciplined analysis.

THE INVISIBLE ADVANTAGE

As you can easily see, these graphs can be quite useful for projecting prices. They have great power for the investor, because they can reveal a trend that is invisible to others, thus giving him a great advantage.

In the present case, the local people who live near D think it's only worth around $1,800 per acre. I know that I'll get at least $2,200 for it though.

Based on my graph, I am certain to achieve this, whereas without the graph, I might have been talked into letting it go for considerably less.

Distance analysis is surprisingly accurate!

AND NOW TIME

Time analysis is used in the same way as distance analysis was, except that now our problem is to predict the future price of a piece of property. This analysis is usually much less accurate than distance analysis, for two reasons.

First, nobody can really predict the future. Any catastrophe can happen, especially in the short term, which might adversely affect the growth rate in the price or demand for land. An example is a recession.

Second, predicting the future price of a specific property requires either a history of prior sales for that exact parcel or a reliable set of comparable sales reaching back several years. Even with today's tools, that level of precision is difficult to achieve and often produces results that are less useful than expected. Rather than attempting to forecast the price path of a single parcel, time-based analysis is far more effective when applied to broader markets—such as an entire county, region, or state—where long-term trends become clear.

Today, the data for this type of analysis is readily available. Historical and current land price information can be obtained from sources such as the U.S. Department of Agriculture, state departments of agriculture, university land-grant extension services, and public real estate databases. Many counties also publish sales data, assessed values, and transaction histories through online GIS and property records systems. These sources make it possible to track long-term land price trends with far greater ease and accuracy than was once possible, while still serving the same purpose: revealing the direction and momentum of land values over time.

An example of time analysis is shown by the graph below. This shows the average price of country land in dollars per acre for the state of Colorado up to the year 1980. The dashed lines show two possible extrapolations to the year 1983. The lower, or pessimistic curve, still shows the average price of Colorado land tripling in value between about 1977 and 1983, or in a space of only six years. And remember, this is only the performance of average land.[1]

Your parcels, selected by the procedures outlined in this report, ought to do at least twice as well. That is, they should triple in price in about three years. The upper, optimistic curve shows land prices at around $980 per acre in 1983!

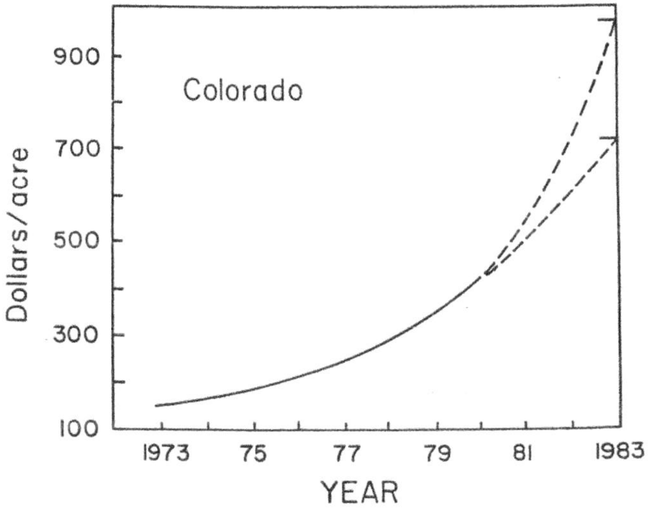

1 This example is intended to illustrate method, not to predict specific future prices.

I will show you exactly how it can be used to greatly increase your profits in the next chapter. Combined with a low initial price, leverage becomes a very powerful tool for reaping big profits.

What can be expected from low-priced land which is to become sought-after vacation land? You might be able to guess this by analyzing the demand for such land over some time period.

The point is that it will not increase in value uniformly. Before the area becomes fashionable, there is often nearly zero demand for it because, as we have said, this type of land is frequently nearly useless for anything else. Land like this does not sell or change owners very often because of low demand—and the low prices may stay nearly the same for many years. However, when a trend towards purchases for vacation or second home purposes begins to develop, prices will begin to climb.

At first this increase will be slow—and it is at this time that we seek to buy. Later, the price rises will be rapid and quite large. The rule-of-thumb for all land purchases is that they should triple in price in three to four years.

For vacation land, we expect the same thing, on the average. What this means is that instead of tripling in just the three years immediately after you bought it, it might increase by a factor of four over four to five years.

Either way you will win in a big way, but you might really clean up if your timing is right.

Let's consider the last case as an example—that is the case where we expect a fourfold increase in price over five years, but this increase is not uniform.

Suppose it goes like this[2]:

Year	Price/Acre	% Increase
1982	$175	0

2 All prices in this example reflect market conditions at the time of analysis.

1983	$175	0
1984	$220	26
1985	$250	43
1986	$700	300

Would you expect to profit by 300% in this example? The answer is "yes" if you paid cash. If you paid cash, you would have better than tripled your money. Very good for you!

But with the leverage that proper financing can provide, you could have done much better. Suppose you bought this land with only 12½% down—or $21.88 per acre—with the balance to be paid off in equal installments over ten years at 8% interest on the outstanding balance.

You would have invested a total of only $124.75 per acre in it and this would have been spread over a five-year period. The percent profit is now 461%—and that beats the 300% on the cash deal by a large factor. In Chapter 13 I show you exactly how this leveraged deal can be done.

But you could have done even better than that! The secret to even greater profits is in timing. In the above example, your investment made you exactly zero money in the first year. Suppose you had waited until around late 1983 or early 1984, after prices had begun to increase? You would have made close to the same large profit margin, but you would have tied up your money for only a little more than three years. Your profit percent per year would have been much greater. You would be making profits at a faster rate, and therefore, you would be able to recycle your capital into additional properties more quickly.

This is the real power of time and distance analysis when they are used together. They help you decide not only where to buy, but when to buy. By purchasing just ahead of rising demand—and not too far ahead—you can sharply increase both the speed and the efficiency of your wealth-building efforts.

In the following chapters, we will put these tools to work in practical ways that allow you to acquire more land, with less money, and at precisely the right moments.

CHAPTER 12

VACATION LAND

There's Gold in Them Thar Hills (And Also in Them Thar Lakes and All the Property Nearby!)

The byword here is that low prices lead to huge profits. Why low prices? Because most vacation land was close to useless for anything else before it became vacation land.

Some of the finest ski country in Vermont was, not so long ago, very rugged timber land—sometimes too rugged to make it very profitable even for timber. Much of that land could be bought for $150 to $200 per acre not too many years ago. In choice locations, it now sells for $1,000 to $1,500 per acre—and that's before roads and utilities.

This story has been repeated many times over across the nation. You can bet that there are some similar places where land prices are rapidly escalating, or are ready to begin climbing, right in your own state.

VERY LARGE PROFITS RESULT FROM LOW PRICES COMBINED WITH LEVERAGE

We will examine the mechanics of leverage—and exactly how to use it to multiply profits—in the next chapter on financing. For now, it is enough to understand the principle. Leverage is the use of other people's money to control valuable land with a relatively small cash investment of your own.

In most cases, that "other people's money" comes directly from the landowners themselves. The objective is to purchase land at a favorable price with a modest down payment, while financing the balance over a long term at a reasonable interest rate. If the land then doubles or triples in value within a few years, your actual cash investment—the down payment plus carrying costs—has increased many times over.

This is leverage at work. Used correctly, it accelerates progress toward substantial wealth. It is the central strategy of this book, and it will be developed in detail in Chapters 13 and 14.

TIMING, DEMAND, AND POPULATION GROWTH

Land should not be purchased until prices have clearly begun to rise. Buying too early—before demand has revealed itself through rising prices—introduces unnecessary risk. Rising prices are the first reliable signal that demand is real and developing. Without that confirmation, a purchase rests largely on speculation, and speculation can tie up capital for years with little to show for it.

Our objective is not modest gains. Our objective is large, decisive profits. That means seeking out locations where demand is already emerging and positioning yourself just ahead of it—not years in advance, and not after prices have already run away.

Once you have identified a promising area, careful observation becomes essential. Price movement should be monitored closely, because timing matters as much as location. The right land purchased at the wrong time can produce disappointing results; the right land purchased at the right moment can produce exceptional ones.

So where do you begin looking for areas where demand is forming?

One of the most reliable starting points is population movement. Areas that are gaining people are gaining demand—demand for housing, recreation, services, and eventually land. Today, this information is far easier to obtain than it once was. Population trends can be reviewed online through U.S. Census Bureau data, state demographic offices, and regional planning agencies, often broken down by county and even by municipality.

Counties with consistently strong population growth deserve closer attention. Growth may be driven by vacation and second-home demand, by industrial expansion, or by the outward push of nearby metropolitan areas. The cause matters less than the fact of growth itself because population growth ultimately translates into increased pressure on land.

Once a promising county has been identified, the next step is to study land patterns within it. Plat books and county GIS mapping systems allow you to examine parcel sizes, ownership patterns, access roads, and the direction of subdivision and development. Using these tools, you can apply the time-and-distance analysis described in Chapter 11 to identify where rising demand is likely to move next.

To stay informed, it is also wise to monitor local information sources. County newspapers—many of which are now available online—often report land transactions, development approvals, zoning changes, and infrastructure projects. Classified listings and online land-sale platforms provide additional insight into asking prices and market sentiment.

Taken together, these tools allow you to replace guesswork with observation, and speculation with informed judgment. This is how timing is improved, risk is reduced, and profits are magnified.

Population growth has always been one of the strongest indicators of where future land demand will develop. Regions experiencing sustained in-migration tend to see increased demand for recreation, retirement, and second-home properties—often well before prices fully reflect that demand.

In recent decades, growth patterns have shifted, but the underlying principle remains unchanged: people move first, prices follow.

In the early 2020s, states in the South and Mountain West have continued to attract strong population inflows, driven by lifestyle preferences, remote work flexibility, and business migration. Many of these same states also continue to offer comparatively lower average land prices than long-established coastal or metropolitan regions.

Here are representative average land values per acre[1] for several lower-cost states, based on recent USDA and national land-value surveys:

New Mexico	~ $2,500
Oklahoma	~ $2,800
Wyoming	~ $2,900
Texas	~ $3,000 to $3,500
Arkansas	~ $3,500 to $4,000

Several states with comparatively moderate land prices also continue to experience population growth, expanding infrastructure, and rising recreational and retirement demand. This combination—low entry prices followed by increasing demand—has produced some of the most profitable land investments in every period.

Prices today may be higher in absolute terms than they were years ago, but the principle has not changed. The greatest gains still accrue to those who recognize developing regions early, before land becomes widely sought after and prices fully reflect demand.

Vacation land yields extraordinary profits because it begins as low-value land and becomes high-demand land. The change occurs gradually, driven by population movement, access, and shifting use. Those who recognize the transition early buy cheaply. Those who wait buy dearly. The difference is not luck. It is observation, timing, and action.

1 Values reflect broad statewide averages for rural and agricultural land; individual parcels may vary widely.

CHAPTER 13

FINANCING

Using Someone Else's Money to Leverage Yourself into Huge Profits

The best way to discuss financing is by an example with typical, and for today, very realistic terms. Here is how a deal might go down.[1]

1. You have located a lovely, well-placed plot of 10 acres and contacted the owner.
2. He is in the mood to sell and asks $1,000 per acre—cash.[2]
3. You tell him immediately that cash is impossible for you.[3] You must have something more like 10% down and 9% interest with a term of 20 years.
4. He will say no.
5. You can leave him to think about it for a few days or weeks.
6. If he calls you back, you know that he hasn't had a better offer and you can deal with him.
7. After several more meetings or phone calls, you find that you cannot shake his price.
8. Now this price you know is just the going rate because, in the meantime, you've found and analyzed a couple of comparables.
9. So you'll have to seek your bargain in the financing

---

1 The specific interest rates and terms available will always vary with time and market conditions, but the structure of the deal—and the effect of leverage—remain the same.
2 Everyone asks for cash.
3 Even if it is possible, don't do it! I'll show you why in a moment.

terms.

10. The two of you finally reach agreement on a 12% down payment with the balance financed for 15 years at 9½%. This is truly a good bargain as you shall see below, even though the contract price is still $1,000 per acre.

FIXED PRINCIPAL PAYMENT FINANCING

Let us suppose that you have done your Time/Distance Analysis well and you smell increasing inflation coming down the pike in several months or next year. In addition, you have noticed the rate of development is increasing and it's only around 8 or 10 miles down the road from your currently interesting parcel.

The owner is aware of this, of course, but uncertain that development will actually arrive at his place. That's why he is unshakable on his asking price.

You have analyzed the direction of development, however, and you think it's a very good bet that the place will be in high demand within a few years. All-in-all, you conclude that it is reasonable to expect to sell in 2 to 3 years for $2,500 per acre, thus raking in a handsome profit.

You and the owner agree to semi-annual payments of principal and interest. Your contract price will be:

Contract price = 10 acres x $1,000 = $10,000

But, your down payment is only 12% of the contract price, or:

Down payment = 0.12 x $10,000 = $1,200

This will leave a loan balance, after closing the deal, of:

Loan balance (after closing) = $10,000 - $1,200 = $8,800

Now the $1,200 is all the money you need to come up with at closing time. Six months later, of course, you will need to make another installment on the principal and you will have to pay the interest on the unpaid balance.

The loan balance will be paid off twice each year for 15 years, or 30 equal installments:

Principal installment = $8,800 / 30 = $293.33

Now, the interest is paid on the current loan balance at the rate of 9½% per year (0.095) and two payments are due each year, so that each interest payment is actually interest due on the loan balance for only six months. The six-month rate would be half the annual rate, or 0.0475.

The first interest payment is:

Interest (first installment) = 0.0475 x $8,800 = $418.00

Therefore, your total first payment, which is due six months after you close the deal, would be: $711.33.

I personally prefer the fixed principal payment method used in the example above because it is simple, transparent, and easy to control. Over the years, I have deliberately avoided complicated financing structures. Not because they are mysterious, but because they are unnecessary.

In practice, nearly all successful land deals turn on just two features:

- first and foremost, **try to get a long term**; and
- second, and nearly as important, **try to get a low interest rate fixed for the life of the mortgage.**

Both of these features are common and relatively easy to achieve in country land deals, whereas in other types of real estate (houses or apartment buildings) "creative" financing is often simply a disguise for high or variable interest rates. These rates are designed to increase as other interest rates go up, and they rob you of the great shelter advantage of the fixed-rate mortgage in times of increasingly high inflation.

WHAT THE NUMBERS SHOW

To return to our fixed principal payment example, here's what your score card would look like for the first three years of your mortgage, assuming that you closed the deal in January 2020:

Date	Principal	Interest	Total	New Balance
Jan. 20	$1,200.00	$ 0.00	$1,200.00	$8,800.00
Jun. 20	$ 293.33	$ 418.00	$ 711.83	$8,506.67
Jan. 21	$ 293.33	$ 404.07	$ 697.40	$8,213.34
Jun. 21	$ 293.33	$ 390.13	$ 683.46	$7,920.01
Jan. 22	$ 293.33	$ 376.20	$ 669.53	$7,626.68
Jun. 22	$ 293.33	$ 362.26	$ 655.60	$7,333.35
Totals	$2,666.65	$1,950.66	$4,617.31	

So, in the course of three years or 36 months, you have tied up $4,617.31 in your land. Does that seem like a large number? Not really, when you compute it on a monthly basis. Your average monthly payment would have been:

Average monthly payment = $4,617.31 / 36 =
$128.25 per month

Not a large number at all! It's more like what you might pay on a new set of living room furniture rather than on a new car. This is because you have managed to get long-term financing.[4]

NEGOTIATING THE PAYMENT SCHEDULE

This example also shows the advantage of negotiating semi-annual (twice per year) or quarterly (four times per year) payment schedules. Spacing out your payments as far apart as possible is very desirable because if you save for them month-

4 Please note that this number is your average monthly payment. If you are saving monthly in order to meet your semiannual payments, you will have to save a little more in the first year because your interest payments are higher then and a little less in the third year.

ly, as I do, you will be putting that money into a savings or money market account every month. You then collect interest while you are saving for the payments! This effectively reduces your interest rate.

In fact, annual payments would be desirable, but they are ordinarily difficult to obtain.

Obviously, a note of caution is appropriate here. You must have the self-discipline necessary to save monthly for the semi-annual payments. If you can do that, you can rapidly set yourself apart from the vast majority of people who seem to only be able to make required monthly payments, such as for cars, furniture, or TVs, and the like.

BETTER THAN A NEW CAR

Those people who commit $150 or $250 each month to furniture or a car are accepting far harsher terms than yours. They must pay monthly, at high interest, on assets that steadily decline in value.

- They will have to pay the going rate of interest.
- They will have to put about 10% - 20% down.
- Their loans will have to be paid off in three to five years.

The bottom line is that installment financing of consumer goods is a sucker's deal. Not at all like yours, which is a great bargain by comparison and is going to make you rich as well!

So, don't buy a new car for the next three years. Buy 10 acres of land instead. And, if you follow the examples shown here, in 10 years you may be able to buy several new cars.

Let's return to our example to see how rich this little deal made us.

After a short three years, you sell for $2,500 per acre. Your sale contract price is:

Sale contract price = 10 acres x $2,500 = $25,000

Out of this, you must pay off your remaining loan balance of $7,333.35, so that you will have a cash balance on hand of:

Cash balance on hand = $25,000 - $7,333.35 = $17,666.65

Imagine! Seventeen-thousand-six-hundred-odd dollars after only three years and starting with only $1,200.

AVERAGE ANNUAL PROFIT

Let's compute your average annual percent profit. I'm not going to calculate this the way a businessman would, but in the least favorable way: I'm going to include the interest payments as part of your investment, whereas in a business sense, they are properly called expenses.

To compute your profit, just take your current cash balance and subtract off all the money you put into the deal over the years:

Profit = cash balance - total investment = $17,666.65 - $4,617.31 = $13,049.34

People often calculate this profit as a percentage of total investment in order to obtain the total percent profit:

Total percent profit =
(Profit / Investment) x 100 =
($13,049.34 / $4,617.31) x 100 = 282.6%

This is an enormous number. You have come close to tripling your money! Your average annual percent profit is the total percent profit divided by three years—or a whopping 94.2% per year.

Actually, you have done even better than that! First, we did not take into account the interest you earned while saving monthly for your semiannual installment payments. And second, the interest payments are deductible from your other income on your federal income tax return.

How much this second item increases your annual profit depends on your tax bracket. If you are in the 25% bracket, for example, you will receive 25% of your annual interest payments back in the form of a tax refund at the end of the year.

DON'T PAY CASH, EVEN IF YOU CAN!

Now let's see what the numbers would have looked like if you had paid cash. This comparison is important, because many people assume that paying cash is automatically safer or smarter. The numbers tell a different story.

At first glance, this might seem a better deal, because now you don't have to pay any interest. As we shall see, "first glances" are deceiving. The cash deal would have been much worse. Now the score is:

Profit =
sale contract price - purchase contract price =
$25,000 - $10,000 = $15,000

Now it's true that this profit is larger than the $13,000 odd you made on the installment deal, but the truth is that the annual percent profit is much smaller for the cash deal. This is true because your investment is much larger in the case of the cash purchase.

Total percent profit =
($15,000 / $10,000) x 100 = 150%

The annual average percent profit would be one-third of this or only 50% per year. Now that margin of profit looks good in anybody's book, but it's only about half what you can make if you finance using someone else's money.

LEVERAGE AGAIN

This ability of using borrowed money to multiply your profits is called **leverage**. It means that even if you can pay cash (which few of us can do) you should not. Instead, you should seek to finance at as low an interest rate possible and for as long a term as possible.

And, to get these terms, you will not have to work hard. It is quite common to find owners today willing to finance at 9½% for 15 years.

Our example was chosen realistically. This is the real bargain in country land. Owner financing at interest rates considerably less than the inflation rate causes the effect of leverage to be much stronger for country land than for other types of real estate.

A PESSIMISTIC EXAMPLE

Do these numbers and percentages seem impossibly high to you? I assure you that they are not! Many, many people—people just like you and me—are earning percentages just like that in their spare time by simply following the procedures I have outlined previously here.

But if you are still somewhat doubtful, and there is absolutely nothing wrong with being doubtful, let's take another example, this time a much more pessimistic one.

Let's suppose that you do none of the things I recommend—you don't pay attention to value, location doesn't concern you, no time/distance analysis to bother with, and you haven't sought out a single comparable. Let's suppose you choose a piece of land to buy by throwing darts at your plat book and then pay the going rate. You don't negotiate favorable terms, either. Again, let's assume you buy 10 acres at $1,000 per acre, but now you put down 25% with the balance finance at 12½% per year for 10 years.

Not especially good terms, I would say, but even so, let's see what happens. Here's what your purchase looks like:

Purchase contract price	$10,000
Downpayment (25%)	$2,500
Starting loan balance	$7,500
Annual principal payment	$750

Semiannual principal payment $375

In order to compare easily this with the previous example, we shall again assume semiannual installments, with the semiannual interest (six month's worth) being 6¼% (that is one-half of the 12½% annual rate). Now your first three years look like:

Date	Principal	Interest	Total	New Balance
January	$2,500.00	$0	$2,500.00	$7,500.00
June	$375.00	$468.75	$843.75	$7,125.00
January	$375.00	$445.31	$820.31	$6,750.00
June	$375.00	$421.88	$796.88	$6,375.00
January	$375.00	$398.44	$773.43	$6,000.00
June	$375.00	$375.00	$750.00	$5,625.00
TOTALS	$4,375.00	$2,109.38	$6,484.37	

Again, we suppose that you sell after three years. How much can you expect to get for it?

Since you chose this property in a completely random fashion (you threw darts at the plat book!) it is reasonable to suppose that it will increase in value each year only at the national average rate. Back in Chapter 4, I showed a table of values that demonstrated that the national average increase in the value of farmland was 25% annually. Here's what its value would have done during the three years you owned it:

Purchase contract price in January 1982	$10,000
Value at the end of 1982	$12,500
Value at the end of 1983	$15,625
Value at the end of 1984	$19,531

Such is the magic of continually increasing land values! So you sell for $19,531 after three years—and here is your score:

Cash balance on hand =
$19,531 - $5,625 = $13,906.00

Profit = $13,906 - $6,484.37 = $7,421.63

Total percent profit =
($7,421.63 / $6,484,37) x 100 = 115%

Annual percent profit = 115 / 3 = 38%

Now that's not bad at all: 38% per year! It certainly beats savings bonds or even certificates of deposit, but it doesn't even touch the much larger percentages you can make with some effort, as we demonstrated in the earlier example.

There are two morals in these two examples. First of all, you can conclude that it pays to do your homework. A carefully chosen property will always outperform a randomly chosen one by a wide margin.

And second, even if you don't do the homework, the average performance of country land is still very profitable.

EXPENSES

The previous examples are optimistic in the sense that they do not take into account the expenses you will incur when you buy, sell, or hold property. I have not included them because they vary widely depending on your particular circumstances and your buying and selling strategy. Here is a list of the most often encountered expenses:

One-time Expenses

1. **Survey.** If you buy from a long-time owner, his land may not have been surveyed within the last 50 to 100 years. Surveying is the process by which legal boundaries of the land are established, and it is absolutely necessary that you have a modern survey before you buy any piece of land. It is often the practice for buyer and seller to equally share survey expenses, but this is negotiable. The cost might be around $250 to $350 for a 10-acre plot, but varies greatly with the

size of the parcel and the location.

2. **Recording fees.** These are the fees you must pay the county for having the deed and mortgage or trust deed recorded at the County Court House. The buyer always pays. These fees are usually around $75 to $125.
3. **Legal.** When you buy, you may wish to have your purchase contract examined by an attorney, though as you gain experience this becomes less important. If there is any question about "clouds on the title"—possible claims of people other than the owner to partial or full ownership—you must have a lawyer look at the deed. Fees may be around $250, but could be somewhat higher if there are complications.
4. **Title insurance.** A kind of insurance, with a one-time fee of about $250, which will fully compensate you in the event that a cloud on the title develops into a full-fledged thunderstorm. If you have any suspicion that others could have full or partial rights of any kind (mineral rights, for example) you will need this. Your attorney can advise.
5. **Brokerage fee.** If you elect to sell through a real estate agency or brokerage office, you will have to pay their fee, which is usually 10% of the contract price, and always paid by the seller.

In the previous "optimistic" example, the sale price was $25,000, so the brokerage fee would be $2,500 on the sale of the property. This would be your largest expense by far. If your property is properly chosen in the first place, you will probably not need a real-estate agent to sell it for you. Prospective buyers will be ringing your telephone ever more frequently as your land comes into ever higher demand.

Some Annual Expenses

1. **County real estate taxes.** These can vary enormous-

ly from what I call exorbitant: $25 to $50 per acre per year; to quite cheap: around $1 per acre per year. The cost most certainly depends upon the use to which the land is, or could be, put, with the highest taxes for land zoned for commercial purposes or for high-density housing, such as condominiums or apartment buildings, and the lowest taxes for vacant land. Also, some counties levy high taxes, while neighboring ones may be much less demanding.

2. **Cosmetic.** This would include annual weed cutting, fence mending, tree trimming, and the like. It is important to keep your property looking pretty.
3. **Mileage on your car.** Don't forget to record it every time you visit your property, even if only for your own pleasure. Why? For your income taxes, that's why.

Though there may be other expenses you might encounter along the way, these are the most important ones. Remember to keep good records of all your expenses, no matter how small, since they are deductible from your profits when determining your income or capital gains taxes in the year that you sell.

In addition, if you can derive any rental income from your land, then your expenses are deductible directly from your income on an annual basis.

Expenses are real, and they must be respected. They do not change the central conclusion. When land is bought correctly, financed intelligently, and sold into rising demand, the effect of leverage overwhelms these costs.

That is why financing is not a detail. It is a multiplier. It determines how much land you can control, how fast you can move, and how often you can repeat the process.

In the next chapter, we will take this further and examine additional financing methods that allow you to expand faster while committing even less cash of your own.

CHAPTER 14

BUYING AND SELLING STRATEGY

Buy on Terms—Sell for Cash

The alert reader will have noticed in the last chapter that in the two examples given, we always bought the land on installment terms—in fact, we sought the easiest possible terms—but we always sold for cash.

Selling for cash is what produced those healthy entries on the score cards labeled "cash balance on hand." This is, of course, the very best possible strategy: buy on the easiest available terms—the lowest down payment, the smallest interest, and the longest term—and after your land has doubled or tripled in value, sell for cash. This technique will result in the most rapid accumulation of capital for you.

PYRAMIDING: A ROUTE TO GREAT WEALTH

Of course, when you sell for cash, you will immediately seek to reinvest that hefty profit in a new parcel of land. In all likelihood, you will have your eye on a couple of interesting prospects already—and you will have already done all or nearly all the homework.

This process of reinvesting your profits is called **pyramiding** and it works something like this:

- You buy the first property and hold it for, say, three years, then sell.
- With those profits you can acquire two new parcels.
- After six years, four pieces.
- And so on.

Obviously it won't work exactly this way because of differences in timing on different parcels or because you might choose to buy one larger or more costly property in the fourth year. But you get the picture. The idea of pyramiding is to plough back your profits into new deals as soon as possible.

This is most important in the early years because it takes some time for the pyramiding process to build up speed. At first it doesn't seem as though you're moving very fast, but after a few years you can be "home free," and moving right along toward new riches.

Here is an example of how pyramiding can produce wealth. First, we need to understand two terms.

At any given time your **equity** is that amount of cash, exclusive of interest and other expenses, that you actually have invested. Normally it will be the sum of your down payments plus all your principal payments. Equity represents the portion of the land's value that you have actually paid for.

The value of your **holdings**, however, is much larger. It is the market value of all property you control.

Control is the key word. Leverage allows you the control of a property of much greater value than the down payment plus principal you have invested. With a small equity, you control holdings of large value.

In this example, we assume that you stay fully invested all the time. You probably cannot do this because of timing and other considerations, such as you may not always find a suitable new parcel at just the time the old one is sold. Also, you will incur some of the expenses listed in the last chapter. All of this will impact your effective annual profit.

Let us suppose you are able to average something like 55% per year. After a few years experience, you probably can exceed this, though at first you may do less well.[1] I will work this example for a beginning equity of $3,000. That's approximately what you would have on a deal with $1,200 down, and average $150 monthly principal payments after one year.

---

1 Remember our pessimistic example in the last chapter. There we achieved around 38% per year without even trying.

Even though you may acquire properties with only say 12½% down, you will be making principal payments regularly. That means you are continually increasing your equity, so that half way through, at the end of 1½ years, your average equity might be more like 20%.

In this example, I will assume an average equity of 20% at any given time. That means that the value of your holdings will always be five times equity. Both equity and holdings grow at 55% per year. Here is how that pyramid would grow:

Time	Equity	Value
Beginning	$3,000	$15,000
End of 1st Year	$4,650	$23,250
End of 2nd Year	$7,207	$36,035
End of 3rd Year	$11,172	$55,860
End of 6th Year	$41,602	$208,010
End of 9th Year	$154,919	$774,595
End of 12th Year	$576,900	$2,884,500

This table shows two things:

1. First, that you could be worth more than half a million dollars while controlling nearly three million dollars worth of property after only about 12 years.
2. Second, and perhaps most important, the early years show slow growth compared to the later years and so it is crucial to reinvest all profits promptly. Many people are unable to build a pyramid of wealth simply because they lack the self-discipline to reinvest during the early years.

THE SILK STOCKING TRADE

In order to sell for cash, you need access to the people who have it. Here, at least initially, a carefully selected real estate broker can be of great value to you. He probably sold a home in the million dollar range fairly recently to the very people you are looking for. They will be middle-aged and rather wealthy, but they will have made their money recently. They have worked hard and now they feel that they can begin to relax somewhat and enjoy a place in the country. Initially, they may just put up a stable and keep some horses, but ultimately they may build a retirement home on it. Like all people of good sense, they want to combine their pleasure with a sound investment.

I call these people the "silk stocking set" and a broker who has gained their confidence—and can introduce your property to them—is very much worth his 10%.

It will be time to go looking for such a broker after three or four years, when you have one or two properties for sale. The ideal broker is, first of all, one who has specialized in the sale of very high quality homes and he may have sold a few pieces of country land as well.

You do not want someone who has primarily specialized in land sales because then you will just have to get in line behind all the rest of his clients. What you are doing is offering the broker a way to expand his business into a new (for him) area.

Under these circumstances, most brokers will leap at the opportunity thus presented. Be aware, too, that you are interviewing him, not the other way around.

Hopefully a mutually beneficial relationship will develop and you will both profit handsomely.

YOU CAN FINANCE THE SALE TOO

As I said just above, the best of all possible sales for you is the one for cash. Nevertheless, it may sometimes become necessary for you to finance a sale for your buyer. You should be quite willing to do so, but be certain that you and the buyer negotiate terms that are very much in your favor compared to the terms under which you yourself bought the land. This will guarantee you a positive cash flow during the term of your sale.

Cash flow is simply the difference between the money you have coming in and that which you must pay out in a given month or quarter. You want a positive cash flow: more coming in than flowing out. Try to negotiate

- a larger down payment than you paid
- at least a point or two higher interest than you are paying
- a shorter term (much shorter, if you can manage it)

Of these three, I favor making concessions on the interest rate rather than the other two items. I have found that it is a very strong selling point if you can offer an interest rate well below the "going rate," which your buyer will take to mean the commercial going rate. Commercial rates are always much larger than the country land rates—and you know that, but your buyer probably doesn't. Whatever you do, don't hint to the buyer anything regarding the terms under which you purchased the land.

The best way to discuss financing your sale is by example. Recall the piece of property you bought in Chapter 13, as shown by the optimistic example. You bought a $10,000 property with $1,200 down, and the balance financed at 9½% for 15 years, with semiannual principal and interest payments. In that example you sold after three years for $25,000 cash.

Now let us suppose that you sell for the same price, but now you must finance the sale. You negotiate with the buyer for 25% down, 11% interest, and a term of 4 years for payment. To make the comparison simple, we will again assume semiannual installments, though you should try for a quarterly or even a monthly payback schedule. After closing the sale, here are some interesting beginning numbers:

Downpayment due you = $25,000 x 0.25 = $6,250

Loan balance due you = $25,000 - $6,250 = $18,750

Semiannual principal due you = $18,750 / 8 = $2,343.75

(There are 8 semiannual payments spread over the 4-year period commencing six months after the closing date.)

First interest payment due you =
$18,750 x 0.055 = $1,031.25

Meanwhile, you must continue to pay off your obligation to the person from whom you originally bought the land. This payout goes according to the same schedule as shown by the table in Chapter 13. However, your payments will be much smaller than your income from your buyer. The details are shown in the following table, where I have rounded off the amounts to the nearest dollar:

OUTFLOW			INFLOW		
Date	**Total**	**Balance**	**Total**	**Balance**	**Net Cash Flow**
Jan. 20	$642	$7,040	$6,250	$18,750	$5,608
Jun. 20	$627	$6,747	$3,375	$16,406	$2,748
Jan. 21	$614	$6,453	$3,246	$14,063	$2,632
Jun. 21	$600	$6,160	$3,118	$11,719	$2,518
Jan. 22	$586	$5,867	$2,989	$9,375	$2.403
Jun. 22	$572	$5,573	$2,860	$7.031	$2,288
Jan. 23	$558	$5,280	$2,731	$4,688	$2,173
Jun. 23	$544	$4,986	$2,602	$2.344	$2,058
Jan. 24	$530	$4,693	$2,473	$0	$1,943
TOTAL CASH ACCUMULATION = $24,371					

In this table, the figures in the *Total* columns are the interest plus principal, calculated by the same method shown in

Chapter 13. The *Net Cash Flow* is, of course, just your total inflow less your total outflow.

Note that you can accumulate $24,371 in cash during the 4½ years of financing. At the end of that period, you only owe $4,693 (last entry in the *Outflow Balance* column) on your old loan, so after paying it off you have a very tidy $19,678 cash on hand for reinvestment.

Also, you didn't have to make any supplementary payments from your other income. In practice, you would have reinvested some of this cash, probably after only a year or two, in order to continue the growth of your pyramid.

These examples are fairly conservative. Following the practices outlined in this book, and with a little effort and reasonable attention to your homework, you should be able to make very similar deals with approximately the same results.

To summarize the conclusions to be drawn from this chapter, you can state that cash sales will result in the most rapid growth of wealth for you, but you can also finance your sales and still make out very well indeed, if you negotiate the proper terms.

CHAPTER 15

WRITING A CONTRACT

Also Deeds, Notes, Closing Statements, and the Like

For me, this is the least interesting part of the entire business. It is also one of the most important. If you intend to buy and sell land without unnecessary trouble, you must understand how these documents work and what they mean.

If you use an attorney, he will prepare the documents for you and advise you on their proper use. If you buy or sell through a real-estate brokerage firm, the broker will usually prepare the necessary papers. Even so, you should never sign anything you do not understand.

You must also be clear about one essential fact: a real-estate agent or broker legally represents the seller. He cannot, by law, represent both parties in the same transaction. Many brokers will try to appear helpful to both sides, and some are genuinely well-intentioned, but their legal duty is to the person who pays their fee.

Always remember that the seller pays the commission. That fact alone determines where the broker's primary loyalty lies.

This does not mean that every broker is dishonest or out to take advantage of you. Quite the contrary. A good broker can be useful and, in some situations, very valuable. But when you approach a brokerage firm as a buyer, you must be knowledgeable enough to read contracts and related documents with understanding and confidence.

That is the purpose of this chapter.

SALE CONTRACTS

The **Sale Contract** is the first document you will encounter. I will discuss it here as though you were the buyer examining a Sale Contract that has been presented to you. Later, when you become a seller, you will either prepare a similar document yourself or have one prepared on your behalf.

These are among the most important papers you will ever sign. A sale contract legally commits you to the purchase or sale of a specific parcel of land and sets forth the exact terms and conditions under which that transaction will take place.

In addition to price and financing, the contract often incorporates other provisions required by state law. Every state has an association of real-estate brokers—commonly known as "realtors"—usually headquartered in the state capital. These associations typically publish standardized, approved contract forms that comply with the land-transfer laws of the state.

It is a sound practice to contact the association in your state and obtain a complete set of these forms. Read them carefully. Familiarity with their structure and language will make you far less dependent on others and far less likely to encounter unpleasant surprises later.

Names

The sale contract begins by clearly identifying the parties involved—the seller and the buyer—and stating that they are entering into an agreement for the transfer of a specific parcel of real estate.

This is followed by a description of the property itself, beginning with the county and state in which the land is located. The description may be the full legal description as it appears on the deed or Certificate of Title, though this is not always the case at the time the contract is written.

If a full legal description is not yet available, the description provided must still be sufficiently clear that an ordinary person could locate the property and understand its approximate boundaries. Precision here is important. Ambiguous or careless descriptions invite confusion later, and confusion in real estate transactions is rarely harmless.

Description

The property description should also include a statement of approximate size. A phrase such as "50 acres, more or less" means exactly that: the parcel is understood to be approximately 50 acres—not 10 or 90—with the final, exact figure to be determined by a survey. A modern survey may reveal, for example, that the true size is 49.83 acres.

A current survey, performed by a registered land surveyor, legally establishes the precise boundaries and acreage of the property. Once completed, that survey becomes part of the legal description shown on the deed and Certificate of Title.

Approximate descriptions are most common when purchasing land from a long-time owner who has never commissioned a modern survey. In such cases, it is essential that the contract clearly state that the final legal description, as shown on the Certificate of Title, will govern—and that it will be incorporated into the Sale Contract when available.

As the buyer, you should also insist that the title be acceptable to you, or insurable to your satisfaction. This condition should be stated explicitly in the contract.

When the Certificate of Title and/or Abstract is delivered, any uncertainty—even a small one—regarding ownership, easements, liens, or other possible claims should give you the right to void the contract. The requirement that title meet your personal approval is not a formality; it is a safeguard, and it belongs in writing as a condition of any agreement based on an approximate description.

Price

Next comes the statement of price. This may be expressed as a single figure for the entire parcel—for example, "fifty-five thousand, two hundred fifty dollars"—or as a per-acre price, such as "three hundred twenty dollars per acre, as determined by the Hanley survey."

The second form is typically used when the contract is written before a modern survey has been completed and both buyer and seller have agreed in advance on the surveyor who will establish the final acreage. Naming the surveyor directly in the contract avoids confusion later. Otherwise, disputes can arise over which survey governs—the current one, or an old survey recorded decades ago in the courthouse.

Older deeds often rely on landmarks that no longer exist or have shifted over time: "the old oak tree," "the center of the stream bed," and similar descriptions that invite ambiguity. Streams change course. Trees disappear. Acreage can vary substantially depending on which survey is used. Good contracts eliminate guesswork. Every reference should be specific.

The price section may also state that a certain amount accompanies the contract as earnest money, which is credited toward the down payment at closing.

Earnest money serves as evidence of the buyer's good faith. It signals serious intent and temporarily secures the agreement. At closing, this deposit is applied against the agreed down payment.

In most states, earnest money may not be mixed with the seller's funds or the broker's operating accounts prior to closing. For this reason, many brokers—and many experienced sellers—will not deposit or cash an earnest money check until the transaction is completed. These safeguards exist to ensure that the buyer's deposit is promptly returned if the deal fails to close for any legitimate reason.

Statement of the Financing

Next comes the statement of financing. This section sets forth the essential terms of the loan: the balance remaining after the down payment, the interest rate to be paid on the unpaid principal, and the length of the term.

The financing clause must also specify the repayment schedule in clear terms. For example: "the balance of $34,000 payable in equal quarterly installments over a period of fifteen years, commencing on the twelfth day of August"—that date being exactly three months after closing, when the first quarterly payment becomes due—"and continuing thereafter at three-month intervals until the balance is fully paid."

At this point, the buyer should insist on including a **prepayment privilege.** This provision grants the buyer the right to pay down or retire the loan early, in whole or in part, without penalty. A typical clause might read: "The buyers reserve the right of full or partial prepayment at any time, without penalty, with interest adjusted to the date of prepayment."

This privilege is essential. If you sell the property before the loan term has expired—as you often will—you must be able to pay off the remaining balance cleanly and without additional cost. Without a prepayment clause, an otherwise profitable deal can become unnecessarily complicated or expensive.

Security

Next comes the statement describing how the loan is to be secured. In most cases, this is accomplished by providing that two documents will be executed at closing.

- The first is a **promissory note,** which serves as written evidence of your debt to the seller.
- The second is a **deed of trust,** which secures that debt by placing a lien on the property.

These documents work together. The note establishes the obligation to repay. The deed of trust protects the seller by tying that obligation directly to the land.

A typical clause might read:

> *The seller agrees to finance a portion of this purchase in the amount of $34,000, such indebtedness to be evidenced by a negotiable purchase-money promissory note, and secured by a first deed of trust on the property, payable on or before a specified date at the agreed interest rate on the unpaid balance.*

It is good practice to include your no-penalty prepayment privilege directly on the note itself, along with a clear statement of the payment schedule. This avoids confusion later and ensures that the terms of repayment are unmistakable.

The lender may also insist on a nontransferability clause. This provision states that the note may not be assigned or passed on to a subsequent buyer. Instead, it becomes "due and payable upon sale of the real estate securing the debt."

In practical terms, this means that if you later sell the property, you must pay off the note in full at that time. This condition is common in owner-financed land deals and should be understood clearly before you sign.

DEEDS

A **deed** is a written document that transfers title to real property from one party, called the **grantor**, to another party, called the **grantee**. In practical terms, your ownership of land is established when the previous owner formally grants that ownership to you through a deed.

Once executed, the deed is recorded at the county courthouse by an official commonly known as the **recorder of deeds** (or a similar title, depending on the jurisdiction). By examining these records, one can "search the title" and trace each successive owner of a parcel of land back through time, often to the earliest settlement of the county.

The deed is among the oldest instruments in the history of land ownership under the English common-law system. Its use became widespread following the enactment of the Statute of Frauds, which arose after the decline of the feudal system under which ultimate ownership of land resided with the Crown.

The Statute of Frauds required that any transfer of land—or any grant of ownership from one person to another—be evidenced by a written document. All nonwritten evidence, regardless of circumstance, was rendered legally insufficient. This marked a major turning point in the law of property. It greatly reduced the ability to defraud the uneducated or illiterate, and it made disputes over land ownership far easier to resolve in court.

There are many different types of deeds, some of which serve very specialized legal purposes. Most buyers will encounter only a few common varieties, and there is no need to examine the others here.[1] Regardless of type, all valid deeds share certain essential elements:

- The **parties are identified**—the grantor and the grantee—and both must be legally capable of entering into a contract.
- **A consideration is stated.** In many states this is expressed symbolically, using language such as "for the sum of ten dollars and other good and valuable consideration," even when the actual price is much higher. Some states, however, require the true purchase price to be stated on the deed.
- A clear **statement of conveyance** is included, such as: "We, the grantors, do hereby grant and convey unto the grantee, his heirs and assigns forever…"

1 Readers interested in a deeper treatment may consult the book by Weich, reviewed in the Resources chapter.

- A **description of the land** is provided. This should be the full legal description based on the most recent survey.
- **Any reservations or restrictions are listed.** These may include easements for roads or utilities, rights-of-way, or liens securing payment for labor or materials. Such liens are commonly known as mechanic's liens.
- **The document is properly executed**—that is, dated and signed by the grantor in the presence of a third party who can attest to the authenticity of the signature, typically a notary public.

It is essential for the buyer to understand that ownership is not fully transferred until the deed has been recorded. Signing and notarization alone are not sufficient. Recording the deed places the transfer on public record and protects the buyer's title against later claims. The recording fee is customarily paid by the buyer.

DEED OF TRUST

In many states, a **deed of trust** is used to secure an obligation owed by the buyer to the seller or lender, and it is particularly well suited to owner-financed land transactions.

A deed of trust involves three parties:

- the buyer or borrower, known as the **trustor**
- the seller or lender, known as the **beneficiary**
- a third party, known as the **trustee**, who is presumed to be neutral

Under this arrangement, legal title to the property is conveyed to the trustee. The trustee holds title in trust for the benefit of the lender until the buyer has fully satisfied the debt according to the terms of the loan.

If the buyer defaults—by failing to make required payments or otherwise violating the terms of the trust deed—

the trustee has the authority to sell the property in order to satisfy the outstanding obligation. This process is generally more direct and efficient than foreclosure under a traditional mortgage, which is one reason deeds of trust are so commonly used in seller-financed transactions.

Although legal title rests with the trustee during the term of the loan, the buyer retains equitable title. This means the buyer has the right of possession and use of the property and may enjoy it fully, so long as those actions do not impair the lender's security interest.

Once the debt has been paid in full, the trustee reconveys legal title to the buyer, and ownership becomes complete and unencumbered.

SATISFACTION PIECE

A **satisfaction piece** is a written statement executed by the lender declaring that a specific indebtedness has been fully paid and satisfied.

As the buyer, you should insist on receiving this document immediately upon making your final payment under the agreed schedule—or upon exercising your right of prepayment if you pay the balance in full. Once this document is executed, you hold clear title to the land, subject only to the proper recording of that fact.

If your debt was secured by a trust deed or mortgage and recorded in the public records, it becomes your responsibility to file the satisfaction piece with the recorder of deeds. Until this is done, the public record will continue to show an outstanding lien, even though the debt has been paid.

It is also sound practice to require the seller or lender to return your original promissory note at the same time. Together, the returned note and the recorded satisfaction piece provide conclusive evidence that the obligation has been extinguished and that your title is free and clear.

CERTIFICATE OF TITLE

A **Certificate of Title** is a document prepared either by the buyer's attorney or by a licensed title abstracting company. Its purpose is to set forth, in one place, the recorded facts affecting ownership of the land.

The certificate includes the legal description of the property, along with a listing of any easements, restrictions, reservations, liens, unpaid taxes, or other claims that appear in the public record. It also discloses any trust deeds, mortgages, or other instruments by which the property may be pledged as security for a debt.

Most important, the Certificate of Title contains a legal opinion. That opinion states whether, based on the public records examined, the seller holds valid title and has the legal right to convey the property to you.

In practical terms, this document answers the essential question every buyer must ask before closing: Does the seller truly own what he proposes to sell, and are there any recorded claims that could interfere with my ownership?

THE CLOSING STATEMENT

Closing takes place at the time and location specified in the Sale Contract, unless another arrangement has been made. This is the moment when money actually changes hands, notes are executed to evidence any indebtedness, and the documents that transfer title are signed.

The closing statement itself is nothing more than a clear accounting of the transaction. It itemizes exactly who pays what, and where every dollar goes. Typically, it will list:

- The total purchase price
- The total down payment
- The amount of earnest money, if any
- Prorated real estate taxes
- Survey fees, if paid by the buyer or shared
- Closing costs, such as notary and administrative fees

- Recording fees
- The amount of the note and trust deed, including interest rate, payment schedule, and term

This document is important not because it is complicated, but because it is final. Once signed, it becomes the financial record of the transaction.

From your standpoint, it is usually to your advantage to delay closing for as long as the contract reasonably allows. During this period, you continue to benefit from the favorable interest rate and long-term financing you negotiated when you bought the property. At the same time, when you are selling, you are often receiving money on firmer or more expensive terms. This difference in timing and terms is one of the quiet ways leverage works in your favor.

CONTRACTS FOR DEED

In its simplest form, a **contract for deed** sets out the agreed terms between seller and buyer. The buyer takes possession of the land and makes payments over time. When the required payments have been completed—or at a specified point—you pay off your own obligation, if any, and convey title to the buyer.

In some cases, you may continue financing part of the sale even after title is conveyed, using a trust deed or similar instrument to secure the remaining balance owed to you.

Contracts for deed can be useful tools, particularly when they allow you to sell a property before you have fully satisfied the terms of your original financing. However, they are not permitted in all states. Before planning to use one, you should verify their legality with a competent attorney or your state's real estate association.

It is also important to understand their limitations. While a contract for deed gives the buyer possession, it often restricts how the land may be used. Activities that could reduce the property's value—such as cutting timber or altering existing improvements—are frequently prohibited. These contracts also tend to allow strict remedies in the event of default. In many cases, all payments made up to that point, including the down payment, are forfeited to the seller and treated as rent.

CROSS YOUR T'S AND DOT YOUR I'S

In this chapter, I have covered only the documents you are most likely to encounter and need to understand. They are not complicated, and they are not meant to intimidate you. But they are important.

These papers determine who owns the land, who controls it, how money moves, and what happens if something goes wrong. When you understand them—even at a basic, working level—you remove uncertainty from the transaction. You are no longer relying entirely on others to protect your interests. You can read what you sign. You can ask the right questions. You can spot problems while they are still easy to correct.

You do not need to become a lawyer. You do not need to draft documents from scratch. What you need is familiarity—enough to recognize what belongs in a contract, what should raise concern, and when professional advice is warranted.

Land investing rewards people who combine sound judgment with steady action. Clear contracts, properly written and understood, make that possible. They turn verbal agreements into enforceable rights, protect your position, and allow you to move forward with confidence rather than hesitation.

Master these fundamentals, and paperwork becomes what it should be: a tool that supports your strategy, not an obstacle that slows you down.

CHAPTER 16

ZERO-CASH DEALS

You Can Start With Nothing!

Back in Chapter 13, we discussed how it is entirely reasonable to earn better than a 90 percent annual return with only a modest, part-time effort. In this chapter, we move into a different category altogether. Here, the discussion turns to transactions that produce profits measured in thousands of percent.

In some cases, the only actual cash you will spend is for gasoline to inspect the property and the routine costs of closing and recording. Other deals require only a token amount of money—so little that it scarcely deserves to be called an investment at all. A number of professionals earn their entire living by locating and executing transactions of this kind. The average individual will encounter them less often, yet they remain entirely within reach.

Whatever approach you eventually adopt as your regular way of doing business, it pays to remain alert for these opportunities. They appear unexpectedly, in ordinary places, and often when least anticipated. When you encounter one, the experience is unmistakable. It feels less like a routine transaction and more like discovering a hidden cache—rare, exhilarating, and immensely rewarding.

GAINING CONTROL OF A VALUABLE PROPERTY AT NO COST TO YOU

What follows is an actual example of a zero-cash deal, described exactly as it occurred—without exaggeration, embellishment, or selective memory. It is presented not as a model to be copied blindly, but as a demonstration of what is possible under the right circumstances.

To make the story more striking, this transaction involved the very first piece of country property we ever purchased. You may be tempted to call it incredible luck. In a sense, it was. Yet it is worth emphasizing that situations like this are not unique. They occur from time to time, and understanding what to look for greatly improves the odds of recognizing one when it appears.

My wife and I had been searching for a country property for several months.Eventually, we came across an attractive corner parcel with frontage on both a paved highway and a gravel road. It lay near a small country town and consisted of a pleasing combination of wooded areas and open meadowland.

Several three- to five-acre lots along the road frontage had already been cleared, suggesting that someone had once considered building homes there. The property appealed to us, and we decided to make an offer—without performing a time-and-distance analysis, without studying comparable sales, and without making any serious effort to determine its true market value. In retrospect, that image of two inexperienced buyers confidently pursuing an investment is more than a little embarrassing.

The tract contained sixty-five acres. The owner was asking $750 per acre. We offered $700 and, after the survey was completed, agreed to a final price of $727 per acre.

We also arranged owner financing, with thirty-three percent down and the balance carried at nine percent interest for ten years. Those terms were written directly into the purchase contract, to which we attached a $500 earnest-money check. The contract was written and was promptly accepted by the sellers.

Because of certain details, the closing was scheduled a couple months later. Up to that point, our only commitment was the $500 earnest-money deposit—and even that had not been cashed, since the selling agent made it a practice not to deposit earnest-money checks until after closing. In practical terms, we had no cash at all invested in the deal.

Before the scheduled closing, a builder—working through a real-estate agent—approached us with an offer of $850 per acre, cash, payable at closing. Those terms were as good as any seller could reasonably expect, and we accepted immediately. The closing on the resale was set for the same day as the closing on our purchase.

On the closing day, the transaction unfolded with remarkable simplicity. In the morning, as buyers, we wrote a check for:

65 acres × $727 = $47,250

Later that same day, as sellers, we received a check for:

65 acres × $850 = $55,250

The gross profit was $8,000. From that amount, we paid a real-estate commission of $4,000 and title and closing costs totaling $112.50. The net profit came to $3,887.50.

And what had we invested? A few telephone calls, several trips into the country to inspect the property, and time spent at two closings. The total cash outlay was perhaps $75. The return on that amount exceeded five thousand percent.

That single transaction was enough to convince us that country land could be a highly profitable part-time pursuit. We have been buying and selling land, in one form or another, ever since. Deals like this do not appear every day, yet the likelihood of finding one improves dramatically when you follow the methods outlined in this book. Yes, the opportunity itself was rare; the structure that made it possible was not.

For my part, this remains the most exciting aspect of the entire activity. Each property carries with it the possibility—however remote—of becoming the next extraordinary opportunity. And when it happens, the experience is unforgettable.

LOW-COST, LOW-RISK OPTION DEALS

An **option** is a contract that gives you the right to purchase a piece of land at a fixed price within a specified period of time. In exchange for a modest payment—which the owner keeps whether or not you proceed—the owner agrees to hold the property for you and to sell it at the agreed price if you choose to act.

During the life of the option, you control the property. You may purchase it at any time within the agreed period by "exercising" the option. If you decide not to proceed, the option simply expires. During this period, the owner may neither sell the land to someone else nor encumber it in a way that interferes with your right to buy.

Options are widely used in many fields, including commodity markets, where prices often hinge on uncertain future events. The logic is straightforward:

- if a particular event occurs, the purchase makes sense;
- if it does not, the obligation quietly disappears.

The option allows you to wait while others speculate.

In land transactions, options are most commonly used when a specific event is expected to increase value—most often a zoning change. The buyer wants the ability to purchase at today's price if the change occurs, while avoiding ownership if it does not. Because zoning decisions are political by nature and subject to pressure, uncertainty is unavoidable. The option limits exposure while preserving upside.

Consider land near the proposed site of a future airport. If built, surrounding land may increase sharply in value, often accompanied by rezoning from agricultural to commercial use. Owners in such areas frequently raise prices in anticipation. An outright purchase under those conditions carries risk. An option, by contrast, allows you to secure the right to buy while waiting for the decision to be made.

When projects of this kind fail to materialize, option holders simply allow their contracts to expire. The cost is limited to the option payment itself—small in relation to the potential gain had the event occurred.

Option prices typically range from two to three percent of the agreed purchase price, with terms often running from one to two years. Longer terms command higher prices, and most provisions are negotiable. As with any land transaction, it pays to bargain: seek the lowest possible option price and the longest practical term.

The central advantage of the option is control. For a small outlay, you control a valuable property for a fixed period without carrying costs or interest. The objective is simple: locate a buyer willing to pay more than your option price. When that occurs, you exercise the option and complete both transactions on the same day.

Used properly, options magnify the power of leverage. They allow you to act decisively while committing very little capital—and they reward those who recognize value before it becomes obvious to everyone else.

THE LISTING CONTRACT AS A ZERO-COST OPTION

Would you like an option that costs nothing at all? Under the right circumstances, a listing contract can serve exactly that purpose.

A **listing contract** is ordinarily an agreement between a property owner and a real-estate brokerage firm. The broker agrees to attempt to sell the property at a specified price within a defined period of time. If a buyer is found, the broker completes the sale and is paid a commission.

Most listing contracts are exclusive. This means the owner agrees not to list the property with any other broker and not to sell it privately during the term of the agreement. Any sale during that period must go through the listing agent.

Now consider what this arrangement represents from a different angle.

If the property can be sold at the listed price during the active period, then whoever controls the sale during that period effectively controls the property. In that sense, the listing contract functions much like an option.

In fact, when a broker lists a property, he has obtained something very close to a free option. If circumstances change—perhaps demand increases, financing becomes easier, or a development decision is announced—the broker can produce a buyer at the listed price and complete the transaction. The owner is bound to sell at that price for the duration of the listing.

For this reason, it is generally illegal—and everywhere unethical—for a broker to list a client's property and then purchase it himself at the listed price. Laws and professional rules exist specifically to prevent brokers from using inside information to profit at the expense of their own clients.

However, what a broker may not do, you may.

As a private individual, there is nothing improper about entering into a listing-style agreement with a property owner. If you can persuade an owner to grant you the right to sell his property at a fixed price for a fixed period, you have effectively secured a zero-cost option.

If, during that period, you locate a buyer willing to pay more than the agreed price, the difference is yours. The owner receives exactly what he agreed to accept. You have created value by finding the buyer.

Under the right arrangement, you may also be entitled to the brokerage commission—often ten percent—paid by the seller. In that case, you are compensated both by the spread between prices and by the commission itself.

All of this can occur without any cash investment on your part.

This technique is not common, and it is not always easy to arrange. But when it can be done, it represents one of the purest forms of leverage available: control without capital, profit without ownership, and risk limited almost entirely to your time and effort.

HOMEWORK AGAIN

By now you will have noticed that most of these deals depend on one simple fact: *you know something the seller does not.*

In practical terms, this usually means that you know a buyer can be found more easily, or at a higher price, than the seller believes. The seller may think his land is slow-moving, difficult to sell, or worth less than it actually is under present or near-future conditions. That difference in perception is where opportunity begins.

Your ability to recognize such situations improves dramatically when you do your homework consistently. This includes

- the time-and-distance analysis,
- studying comparable sales,
- tracking proposed developments, and
- learning where roads, lakes, recreational facilities, or zoning changes are likely to appear.

Information of this kind changes land values long before the changes become obvious to everyone else.

If your homework tells you that a buyer could be found within a reasonable period—six months, for example—you can act with confidence. Under those circumstances, you may be willing to contract for a property on almost any terms, provided the price is right. Even without cash on hand, you can write a purchase contract and include an earnest-money deposit, then set the closing date as far in the future as the seller will allow. That interval becomes your window of opportunity to locate a buyer.

This approach does involve **risk**. If you fail to find a buyer before the closing date, you may be forced to borrow the down payment and cover closing and recording costs under unfavorable terms. At that point, lenders—not you—will dictate the conditions, and they will do so to their advantage.

If that level of risk is uncomfortable, there is a simpler alternative: *do not contract to buy the land—buy an option instead.* With an option, your maximum exposure is limited to the option price. If you fail to find a buyer during the option period, that loss is fixed and known in advance.

In the first case, you may complete a true zero-cash deal.

In the second, you may complete a very low-cost deal.

In both cases, the percentage returns can be extraordinary.

The principle is always the same. Superior information creates control. Control creates opportunity. And opportunity, when acted upon intelligently, produces results far out of proportion to the cash invested.

CHAPTER 17

COUNTRY LAND: WEALTH, SECURITY, INDEPENDENCE

Why It Is The Best Route To Riches Now And For A Long Time To Come

"They aren't making any more of it." Everyone has heard the phrase, and it captures the central fact better than any technical explanation. Land is governed by the simplest and most reliable of economic laws: supply and demand. Demand for land has existed as long as private ownership has existed, and it will continue so long as people need places to live, work, and retreat. The supply, however, is fixed.

Wherever private ownership has been permitted, the price of land has risen steadily over time. This has been true throughout recorded history. In older countries—England and much of continental Europe—land prices have already reached levels where only the very wealthy can afford more than what Americans would consider modest holdings. The same process is now well advanced in the United States.

In America, the supply of desirable land near major population centers is steadily diminishing. As cities expand, they divide and consume surrounding acreage, leaving fewer large parcels and driving prices upward. This process has occurred for generations, and there is no reason to expect it to change. Land prices in such areas have consistently risen faster than the general cost of living, and they continue to do so.

You need only consult a plat book to see this pattern at work. As you move closer to established cities and towns, parcels become smaller, ownership more fragmented, and prices higher. Those ever-smaller divisions reflect a persistent and growing hunger for land—a demand that has existed for a very long time and shows no sign of abating.

ESCAPE FROM THE CITY

People will continue to look for ways to escape the growing burdens of city life. In many areas, the cost of owning property in urban centers has risen to such levels—through taxes, insurance, utilities, and fees—that living farther out and commuting has become the more economical choice. What was once considered an inconvenience is now often a financial advantage.

Cost, however, is only part of the motivation. Many people are also seeking relief from the everyday problems that accompany dense urban living. Crime, congestion, and the steady erosion of public services have made city life less attractive to a growing number of families. Schools are overcrowded and increasingly expensive to support. Police and fire protection often cost more while delivering less. In too many places, residents are asked to pay more each year for services that continue to decline in quality.

By comparison, country living offers both economy and relief. Property costs are lower, space is abundant, and the pace of life is less compressed. For many people, the tradeoff is obvious, and they are acting on it.

For the first time in modern history, population movement has shifted away from a relentless concentration in cities toward surrounding rural and semi-rural areas. This movement is driven by economics, lifestyle preferences, and a desire for greater independence. Once such a shift begins, it tends to reinforce itself. As more people move outward, demand follows—and land prices rise accordingly.

The implication is clear. As people continue to leave crowded urban centers in favor of country and small-town living, the demand for country land will increase. And as demand increases against a fixed supply, prices will continue their long upward climb.

BACK TO NATURE

Land values have also been strengthened—powerfully and persistently—by the continuing movement back toward self-reliance and natural living. Many people want greater control over what they eat, how they live, and the resources they depend upon. Producing food, harvesting materials, and living closer to the land all require one essential thing: land itself.

At the same time, there has been a growing desire for independence from large, centralized systems. Energy costs, utility expenses, and infrastructure fees have risen steadily for decades, often faster than household incomes. In response, people have sought alternatives that place control back in their own hands. Heating with wood, growing food, generating small-scale power, and managing water and resources locally all point in the same direction—toward owning usable land.

What once seemed unconventional has become practical. Self-sufficiency is no longer a fringe idea. It is a deliberate lifestyle choice made by people who value resilience, autonomy, and long-term security. Each year, more individuals and families decide that owning land is the foundation of that independence.

These modern homesteaders—sometimes called survivalists, sometimes simply practical people—are not retreating from society. They are positioning themselves wisely. Their growing numbers represent a steady and durable source of demand for country land, and that demand translates directly into rising values over time.

SUSPICION OF TECHNOLOGY

There has been a growing shift away from the long-held belief that scientific and technological progress automatically produces a better life. While innovation has brought undeniable convenience, it has also introduced complexity, dependence, and uncertainty. For many people, improvements in material comfort have been accompanied by a quiet unease about systems they do not understand and cannot control.

Large-scale technologies now shape daily life in ways that feel distant and impersonal. Decisions affecting energy, food, communication, and infrastructure are made far from the individual, often by institutions that seem unresponsive to local needs. This has fostered a sense of vulnerability rather than confidence.

As a result, many people are deliberately simplifying. They are drawn toward what might be called "first principles" living—greater self-reliance, tangible skills, and direct control over essential resources. This impulse naturally pulls people away from dense urban centers and toward suburban and rural settings, where land provides both physical space and personal agency.

The movement is not a rejection of progress, but a recalibration. It reflects a desire to balance modern convenience with independence and stability. Country land answers that desire directly, offering a practical way to regain control while still participating in the modern world.

SAFETY IN COUNTRY LAND INVESTMENTS

Taken together, the forces discussed above—and the analysis presented earlier in this book—point to one clear conclusion: country land is among the safest long-term investments available. Very little can go fundamentally wrong when land is purchased intelligently and held with patience. It does not deteriorate, it does not become obsolete, and it does not depend on tenants, managers, or complex operating systems to retain its value.

Few investments offer comparable security over long periods of time. Country land stands apart because it is supported by permanent demand, finite supply, and broad social trends that operate independently of short-term economic cycles.

Just as important, it is ideally suited to the average individual. It does not require constant attention, specialized training, or a full-time commitment. For those with limited spare time—or who wish to build wealth alongside another occupation—country land provides a practical and reliable path to independence without the pressures and risks common to more complicated investments.

COUNTRY LAND IS ALSO THE EASIEST

The procedures described in the preceding chapters are genuinely simple. Anyone can learn them. Selecting property for appreciation, arranging financing, and marketing land for resale are all far less complicated—and far less prone to costly error—than most other investment activities. No advanced education or business training is required. What matters is persistence, attention, and the willingness to act.

By comparison, many popular investments are filled with uncertainty. Coins, precious metals, and securities may rise in value, and they may just as easily fall—often suddenly and without warning. Gains and losses arrive unpredictably. To my mind, that resembles speculation more than investment. Some people enjoy that sort of risk. I do not. I prefer investments that either move steadily forward or, in the worst cases, hold their ground.

Real estate occupies that category. And within real estate, country land stands apart.

Broadly speaking, there are three principal avenues available to the individual investor: rental property, commercial property, and country land. Of these, country land is the easiest to enter successfully. It is also the safest, when all factors are considered. You may begin on a modest scale or a larger one, according to your means, without being forced into complexity.

Rental and commercial properties carry disadvantages that are often overlooked. Most significantly, they must be actively managed while you wait for appreciation to occur. Property management is a profession in its own right, and mistakes are costly. Tenants damage property. Vacancies reduce income. Payments arrive late or not at all. Neighborhoods change. These challenges are not occasional inconveniences; they are persistent realities.

Commercial property presents similar difficulties, along with additional burdens such as higher insurance costs, security concerns, and greater exposure to economic cycles. In many cases, the problems associated with these investments are simply the problems of cities themselves.

Competition is also more intense. Many experienced investors operate in these markets full time, and it is difficult for a newcomer to secure truly favorable purchases. Financing, too, is less accommodating. Even where owner financing is available, terms are rarely as generous, and seldom cover the entire purchase price. The balance must be financed through institutional lenders at higher—and often variable—rates, which erodes profitability, particularly during periods of inflation.

Finally, the cost of entry is substantial. Income-producing properties generally require significant capital. Bargains, when they appear, often conceal expensive repairs or structural issues that demand immediate attention.

Country land avoids these complications. It requires no tenants, no repairs, no management staff, and no constant oversight. Its value grows quietly, supported by demand rather than maintenance. For the individual seeking a practical, understandable, and forgiving route to long-term wealth, no form of real estate compares.

MORE REASONS WHY COUNTRY LAND IS THE EASIEST ROUTE TO RICHES

By way of comparison with other forms of real-estate investment, it is useful to summarize the specific advantages that make country land so uniquely attractive.

1. **No special education or technical training is required.** Nearly anyone can develop a meaningful second income—and ultimately real wealth—by applying the straightforward principles outlined in this book. The learning curve is gentle, and the fundamentals are easily grasped.
2. **Country land is forgiving.** Even when mistakes are made, or when research is less thorough than it should have been, time itself often corrects the error. Land has a way of maturing into value. In rental or commercial property, similar mistakes can be costly and sometimes irreversible.
3. **The financing terms are among the best available.** Owner financing at reasonable interest rates and for long terms is common. Deals usually involve only one or two parties, making negotiation direct and manageable. By contrast, other real-estate transactions often require coordination with bankers, insurers, brokers, and sometimes tenants, each adding complexity and constraint.
4. **Large amounts of capital are not required to begin.** Country land exists in every size and price range. Some of the highest percentage returns have come from very small parcels, requiring modest—or occasionally no—cash investment at all.
5. **You can use and enjoy your investment.** For many people, this is the most compelling advantage. Hunting, fishing, hiking, camping, cutting wood, and simply spending time outdoors all become part of ownership. Each property develops a character of

its own, and owners often grow attached to the land they hold. It is difficult to imagine deriving comparable satisfaction from an apartment building or a portion of a warehouse.

6. **The people involved are generally more straightforward.** Country sellers tend to be practical and direct. Negotiations are often conducted without pretense or unnecessary formality. In my own experience, land transactions rarely require dealing with institutional lenders, a fact I regard as a distinct benefit.
7. **Country land can also produce income.** Every parcel has some earning potential, however modest. With a bit of imagination, even limited income streams can be developed, and the act of doing so frequently increases the property's overall value.
8. **Finally, land investing lends itself naturally to partnership.** Spouses, companions, or close friends can learn the process together, each contributing different strengths. The activity itself—reviewing listings, visiting properties, planning future uses—can become a shared pursuit rather than a source of friction. In many jurisdictions, the law itself recognizes joint ownership in ways that reinforce cooperation and continuity.

THE ADVENTURE AHEAD

My hope is that this book has demonstrated just how accessible, resilient, and rewarding country land investing can be—and how naturally it lends itself to building independence, security, and lasting wealth. This is an arena where thoughtful action and steady persistence are consistently rewarded, and where opportunity continues to renew itself for those prepared to recognize it.

The principles you have learned here are not theoretical. They are practical, repeatable, and adaptable to your own circumstances and ambitions.

Review them carefully.

Make them your own.

Apply them patiently and with confidence.

Then step forward. Study the listings. Walk the land. Talk to owners. Trust what you are learning.

Each parcel you encounter carries the possibility of something more, and the pursuit itself becomes part of the reward.

Above all, enjoy the process. You are entering a field where progress is tangible, effort compounds, and the journey is every bit as satisfying as the destination.

APPENDIX I

RECOMMENDED READING

A Select Library for Serious Students of Land and Wealth

There are surprisingly few books devoted specifically to profiting from country land—certainly far fewer than those written about city, commercial, or income property. That imbalance is unfortunate, because a program centered on country land can be every bit as profitable as urban investing and, in many respects, more durable, more flexible, and more personally satisfying.

Part of the reason may be cultural. City investors tend to talk about what they do—and to write about it. Country land investors tend to act. They buy land, improve it, hold it, sell it, and move on. The work speaks for itself.

Over the years, I have read virtually every serious book written on country land investing, along with a number of broader works on real estate, finance, and speculation. The books listed here were chosen not for novelty, but for usefulness. Some are practical references. Others provide strategic perspective. A few offer historical context that sharpens judgment and reinforces first principles.

Markets change. Credit conditions change. Styles and terminology change. The underlying mechanics of land ownership, leverage, inflation, and human behavior do not. These books explain those enduring foundations. Read them selectively, return to them when questions arise, and use them to deepen—not replace—your own thinking.

REAL ESTATE PRINCIPLES AND PRACTICES

by A. A. Ring and J. Dasso; Prentice-Hall

This book is widely regarded as the standard reference for the real estate profession. It provides a thorough treatment of nearly every aspect of the field, from basic principles and property rights to contracts, financing, title, and long-range market considerations. When an unfamiliar term or obscure instrument arises—a rarely used deed, an unusual contract, or a technical point of procedure—it can almost always be found explained clearly here.

I found the chapters on deeds, transfers of title, mortgage financing, liens and easements, and land surveying and property descriptions particularly valuable. Everything in the book is practical, and much of it will eventually prove useful.

REAL ESTATE

by I. E. Weich; Barnes & Noble Books (Harper & Row)

This is also a reference work, though older and more concise than Ring and Dasso. Its chief advantages are its brevity, readability, and portability. Unlike many reference texts, it can be read straight through without effort. While it does not cover every subject in depth—I had to return to Ring and Dasso for a full discussion of contracts for deed—it serves as an excellent companion volume and a convenient working reference.

LAND INVESTMENT: GUIDE TO A SECOND INCOME FORTUNE

by J. A. Dygert; Prentice-Hall, Inc.

This is an encouraging book which I found very interesting and quite easy to read. It proves the main point that I try to make here: namely that anyone can make a "second income fortune" given only that he or she have reasonable common sense and persistence. Dygert is a very clear writer, and always seems able to get his point across. I liked it very much that he doesn't send you straight away into the arms of a broker. He has very good discussions on financing, leverage, and investment strategy. My one complaint is that there is virtually nothing on the documents and instruments you will need to understand.

BUYING LAND—HOW TO PROFIT FROM THE LAST GREAT LAND BOOM

by A. M. Watkins; Quadrangle/The New York Times Cook Co.

I doubt that it will be the "last great land boom" since I believe that opportunities to profit from land trading and investing will extend into the indefinite future wherever and so long as private ownership and free trading are allowed by governments. A very professional book meant for the professional, but useful to us as well. He has produced excellent discussions of traps and pitfalls and how to avoid them, and a fine analysis of financing and how to estimate after tax yields. The main thrust is toward more "close-in" buying thanI am inclined to. Thus he pays a very high price for land which will very soon be rezoned to commercial or high density. This is not for the amateur or beginner!

BUYING COUNTRY PROPERTY

by I. Price; Harper & Row.

This man is quite definitely a broker and a professional. He gives the usual and expected advice in the very early parts of the book. There is a very good list of pitfalls and traps, but then brokers are always motivated to convince you that the sky will surely fall if you don't use their services (their often quite expensive services, thank you). There is really not so much of use in this book compared to several of the others.

PROFITS FROM COUNTRY PROPERTY: HOW TO SELECT, BUY, MAINTAIN AND IMPROVE COUNTRY PROPERTY

by J. H. Koch; McGraw-Hill, Inc.

This is absolutely one of the best books in existence, and it is also the most recent. The author is the publisher of a newsletter on country property. The most out-standing feature is that the book is filled with statistics: everything from decade-long trends in population growths by state to the average rental cost per acre for pasture land. There is a good projection of the coming demand for country land, along with projections for sharply increasing prices. There is a great deal of" how to" advice on selection, improvement, renovation, and resale, etc. A very good discussion on the impact of the growing trends toward environmental regulation on country land prices. This book is very well worth having for the statistics along, even with the long-winded title.

HOW TO REAP RICHES FROM RAW LAND: GUIDE TO PROFITABLE REAL ESTATE SPECULATION

by G. Nicely; Prentice-Hall.

Long-winded titles seem to run in the family. This is a "nice" book of the encouraging "you can do it too even while blowing bubble gum" type. It's a treasury of happy homilies like "always buy under the market," or " keep up your courage, maintain optimism and develop a can-do attitude." It does have a quite good discussion of leveraging and an illuminating comparison with investments in the stock market. The book also includes a Chapter on HUD and its programs.

BUYING COUNTRY PROPERTY

by J. R. Moral; Gardenway Publishing.

More oriented toward the one-time buyer rather than the investor or speculator. There are several good books on "How to buy a farm" which I don't discuss. I include this one as an example, and because it's recent.

THE GREAT AMERICAN LAND BUBBLE

by A. M. Sakolski; Harper & Brothers.

An interesting and exciting story of land-grabbing, speculations, booms and busts from colonial times to the great depression of the thirties. All the key figures are here, and some might surprise you. For example, it is pointed out that even George Washington knew the value of a well-chosen parcel of land. The book presents a region-by-region or state-by-state exposition of settlement, extraction of title, and subsequent division and sale of the land.

THE COMING REAL ESTATE CRASH

by J. English and G. E. Cardiff ; Arlington House.

This book was written with a point of view formed in the frenzy of the California housing market in the final days of the 1979 hyper-inflation. People were actually using houses in the San Francisco Bay area as alternates to paper money which they had lost faith in. The authors liken this specific speculation in local housing to a number of other booms of historical importance, which inevitably were always followed by busts. There is a good discussion of the effects of inflation on real-estate markets. I was particularly interested in, and amused by, a graph showing 1000 years of inflation in England; inflation, in fact, since medieval times, which continues unabated to this very day.

PAPER MONEY AND THE EARLIER THE MONEY GAME

by Adam Smith; Random House.

These are very entertaining books. They are exciting and very literate. They teach one main lesson: that it is always politically easiest to debase the money. In other words, inflation is always the easy way out for government and for individual politicians. As Adam Smith shows, this has been true since Roman times; and probably (even very likely) before if people could only document it. The lesson is that as money becomes more and more worthless, only real property (land !) maintains a store of value. Read these books— they are worth it in information as well as the sheer pleasure of the story.

APPENDIX II

THE IW$ RURAL REAL ESTATE FAST START PLAN

1. **Prepare Your Mindset and Time**
   - Commit to a modest, regular schedule
   - Decide how country land fits your life
2. **Choose Your Target Area**
   - Radius selection
   - Why familiarity matters
   - When distance works
3. **Begin Market Observation**
   - Reading listings
   - Tracking price patterns
   - Learning the "feel" of land
4. **Start Conversations**
   - Owners
   - Agents
   - Neighbors
   - Builders
5. **Structure for Control, Not Ownership**
   - Contracts
   - Options
   - Delayed closings
6. **Stay Patient, Stay Ready**
   - Why most profits come from waiting
   - Why readiness beats activity
7. **Act Decisively When the Right Deal Appears**
   - What "right" actually means
   - Why hesitation kills leverage

Glossary

abstract of title. A compilation of recorded documents affecting a parcel's ownership history and title status. It typically includes deeds, mortgages or deeds of trust, liens, easements, restrictions, and other matters of record.

acreage. The land area of a parcel measured in acres. When acreage is stated as "more or less," it indicates an approximation that becomes exact only after a modern survey.

after-tax yield. The return on an investment after accounting for applicable taxes. Investors use it to compare real estate returns against other investments on an equivalent basis.

appraisal. A written opinion of value by a qualified appraiser, often used by lenders. In land investing, market value is also commonly judged through comparable sales and local demand patterns.

assignment. A transfer of contract rights from one party to another. In land deals, a buyer may assign a purchase contract to a new buyer, subject to the contract's terms and local custom.

beneficiary. In a deed of trust, the lender or seller whose loan is secured by the property.

boundaries. The lines defining a parcel's limits. Boundaries become legally precise through a survey and the legal description that reflects it.

broker. A licensed intermediary who represents a party in a real estate transaction. A broker's legal duties follow the party represented and the brokerage agreement governing the relationship.

certificate of title. A document prepared by an attorney or title company stating the legal description, recorded encumbrances, and an opinion regarding ownership and marketability of title based on public records.

closing. The meeting or process where funds are paid or disbursed, financing instruments are executed, and the deed is signed and delivered for recording, completing the transaction.

closing costs. Transaction expenses beyond the purchase price, such as title work, recording fees, notary fees, survey charges, escrow or settlement charges, and similar administrative items.

closing statement. A final accounting of the transaction showing the purchase price, credits and debits to each party, prorations, fees, financing amounts, and net funds due.

cloud on title. A condition in the record that creates uncertainty about ownership or the quality of title, such as an unreleased lien, an unclear easement, or a break in the chain of title.

commission. Compensation paid for brokerage services, commonly calculated as a percentage of the sale price, as set by contract.

comparables. Recent sales of similar properties used to estimate market value. Comparable analysis often considers location, access, size, topography, utilities, zoning, and demand.

consideration. The value exchanged to form a binding contract or to support a conveyance. Deeds often recite consideration in symbolic form even when the true price is higher.

contract for deed. An installment sale arrangement where the buyer receives possession and pays over time, while title typically transfers later upon meeting specified payment conditions. Terms and enforcement vary by state and by contract language.

deed. A written instrument that transfers title from the grantor to the grantee. Recording the deed places the transfer in the public record and protects the grantee's claim against later disputes.

deed of trust. A security instrument used in many states to secure a loan with real property. It involves three parties—trustor, beneficiary, trustee—and enables sale of the property under specified conditions if default occurs.

default. A failure to perform obligations under a loan or contract, commonly failure to make required payments or to meet covenants stated in the security instrument.

description of property. The identification of the land being transferred. It may be a full legal description or an interim description sufficient to locate and recognize the parcel, later refined by survey and title documentation.

down payment. The portion of the purchase price paid in cash or equivalent at closing, with the remaining balance financed.

due-on-sale clause. A provision making the loan balance due upon sale or transfer of the secured property. It functions as a form of nontransferability tied to ownership change.

easement. A recorded right for a party to use a portion of another's land for a specific purpose, such as access, utilities, or drainage. Easements affect value and use, and they appear in title work.

equitable title. The buyer's beneficial interest and right of possession and use, subject to the lender's security interest, while legal title may be held by another party in a deed of trust structure.

earnest money. A deposit tendered with a purchase contract to demonstrate serious intent. It is typically credited toward the down payment at closing and is commonly handled under rules that protect the buyer if the deal fails for recognized reasons.

encumbrance. A claim, restriction, lien, easement, or other recorded interest that affects title, value, or use of the property.

exclusive listing. A listing contract granting one broker the exclusive right to market a property for a stated term. During the term, the owner typically agrees that sale efforts go through that broker.

exercise of an option. The act of choosing to purchase under an option agreement by meeting the option's stated conditions within the option period.

frontage. A parcel's boundary that borders a road, highway, shoreline, or other feature. Road frontage often influences access, desirability, development potential, and value.

grantor. The party who conveys title through a deed.

grantee. The party who receives title through a deed.

installment payment schedule. The agreed timetable for repaying a financed balance, including payment frequency and due dates, often stated in the note and referenced in the sale contract.

interest rate. The percentage charged on unpaid loan balance, expressed annually unless stated otherwise, forming a major driver of long-term carrying cost.

legal description. The precise description of a parcel used in deeds and title work. It may be metes and bounds, lot-and-block, or other recognized formats, and it is commonly tied to a survey.

legal title. The formal ownership interest recognized in law. In a deed of trust structure, legal title is conveyed to the trustee as security, while equitable title remains with the buyer.

leverage. The use of borrowed funds or structured terms to control a larger asset than cash alone would permit. In land investing, leverage can arise from owner financing, options, delayed closings, and resale timing.

lien. A legal claim against property to secure payment of a debt or obligation. Liens appear in title work and can affect closing, refinancing, and resale.

listing contract. An agreement between a property owner and a broker defining marketing authority, price guidance, term, commission, and other conditions.

mechanic's lien. A lien filed by a contractor, subcontractor, or supplier for unpaid labor or materials furnished to improve property. It attaches to the property and must be cleared for clean title.

metes and bounds. A legal description method using distances and directions, often referencing monuments, corners, and boundary lines.

mortgage. A security instrument used in many states to secure a loan with real property. It functions similarly to a deed of trust but follows a different legal structure and foreclosure process depending on jurisdiction.

nontransferability clause. A provision stating that a loan or note may not be assumed by a later buyer, often requiring payoff upon sale.

notary public. A public official authorized to witness signatures and certify acknowledgments, helping ensure authenticity of execution for recording.

option. A contract giving the option holder the right, within a specified time, to purchase property at an agreed price. The owner is bound to sell under the option's terms if the option is exercised.

option period. The stated time during which an option may be exercised. The owner typically agrees to keep the property available under the agreed price and terms during this period.

option price. The payment made to obtain the option. It is commonly kept by the owner whether or not the option is exercised.

parcel. A distinct unit of land recognized for ownership and conveyance, identified by legal description and tax or record references.

plat book. A map-based reference showing land divisions, ownership boundaries, roads, and parcel identifiers, useful for understanding patterns of subdivision and development.

prepayment privilege. A loan term allowing early payoff in whole or in part, commonly without penalty, with interest adjusted to the payoff date. It supports clean resale and flexibility.

principal. The unpaid balance of a loan, excluding interest.

proration. An allocation of expenses or income between buyer and seller based on time, commonly used for property taxes, rents, and certain fees at closing.

purchase-money promissory note. A promissory note given by the buyer to the seller as part of the purchase price, reflecting seller financing.

raw land. Undeveloped land, often lacking improvements such as buildings, utilities, or paved access. Value is shaped by location, access, zoning, demand, and potential uses.

recorder of deeds. The county official or office responsible for recording deeds and other instruments. Recorded documents become part of the public record affecting title.

recording. The act of filing a deed, deed of trust, mortgage, or related instrument in the public record. Recording establishes priority and provides public notice.

reservation. A right or interest retained or stated in a deed, such as an easement, mineral rights reservation, or other limited interest affecting use.

restriction. A recorded limitation on use, development, or activity on the land, often arising from covenants, zoning, subdivision rules, or specific deed provisions.

rezoning. A change in a property's permitted use classification under local zoning rules. Rezoning can materially affect value, development potential, and market demand.

right-of-way. A type of easement granting passage across land, often for roads, driveways, or utilities.

sale contract. A binding agreement setting price, property description, contingencies, financing terms, closing date, and other conditions for purchase and sale of real property.

satisfaction piece. A written statement by the lender confirming that a recorded debt has been paid. Recording it clears the lien from the public record and supports clear title.

security instrument. A document securing repayment of a loan by giving the lender enforceable rights in the property, such as a deed of trust or mortgage.

simultaneous closing. A purchase and resale closing arranged for the same day, allowing contract control to convert into profit with minimal carrying time, provided all documents, funds, and title requirements align.

survey. A professional measurement of land boundaries and features performed by a licensed surveyor. It produces a definitive basis for legal description and acreage.

tax parcel number. A government identifier used for assessment and taxation. It assists in locating records but does not replace a legal description.

tenant by the entirety. A form of co-ownership commonly available to married couples in many states, treating the couple as a single legal unit for ownership, transfer, and survivorship purposes.

time-and-distance analysis. A practical method of evaluating land based on proximity to towns, roads, employment centers, services, and growth corridors, helping forecast demand and resale potential.

title. The legal right of ownership to property, subject to recorded encumbrances and lawful interests of others.

title insurance. Insurance protecting against certain defects in title existing as of the policy date, based on a title search and underwriting standards.

title search. A review of public records to determine ownership history and recorded interests affecting the property, forming the basis for title opinions and insurance.

trustee. In a deed of trust, the neutral third party holding legal title in trust as security and empowered to act under the deed's terms if default occurs.

trustor. In a deed of trust, the borrower or buyer who grants the deed of trust as security for the obligation.

zoning. Local land-use regulation defining permitted uses and development standards, such as agricultural, residential, commercial, or industrial classifications.

zero-cash deal. A transaction structured so that the investor's required cash outlay is minimal, with profit arising from timing, control, and terms—often through contract rights, delayed closing, and a matched resale.

Index

D

E

If you can dream it,

then you can do it –

and IW$ will show you how!

iWealthSuccess.com

Made in the USA
Monee, IL
04 November 2026

67374649R00089